# Breaking the Silence on NGOs in Africa

Edited by
Nicholas Mwangi & Lewis Maghanga
Kenya Organic Intellectuals Network

Foreword by
Issa G. Shivji

INCLUDES:

*Silences in NGO Discourse:
The Role and Future of NGOs in Africa*
&
*Reflections on NGOs in Tanzania: What We Are, What We Are Not
and What We Ought To Be*

by
Issa G. Shivji

Daraja Press

Published by
Daraja Press
https://darajapress.com
Wakefield, Québec, Canada

ISBN 9781990263675

Cover design: ck nosun

Library and Archives Canada Cataloguing in Publication

Title: Breaking the silence on NGOs in Africa / edited by Nicholas Mwangi & Lewis Maghanga.
Names: Mwangi, Nicholas, editor. | Maghanga, Lewis, editor. | Container of (work): Shivji, Issa G. Silences in NGO discourse. | Container of (work): Shivji, Issa G. Reflections on NGOs in    Tanzania.
Description: "Included: Silences in NGO Discourse: The Role and Future of NGOs in Africa; &, Reflections on NGOs in Tanzania: What We Are, What We Are Not and What We Ought To Be, by Issa    G. Shivji". | Includes bibliographical references.
Identifiers: Canadiana 20230169163 | ISBN 9781990263675 (softcover)
Subjects: LCSH: Non-governmental organizations—Africa. | LCSH: Non-governmental organizations— Social aspects—Africa.
Classification: LCC JZ4841 .C75 2023 | DDC 361.7/7096—dc23

# CONTENTS

# Foreword
## Issa G. Shivji

## BY WAY OF APPRECIATION

I am doubly honored by the Organic Intellectuals Network of Kenya; firstly, because the Network thought it worthwhile to discuss my small book on the *Silences in the NGO Discourse* and secondly because of the invitation to write this Foreword to their reflections on the book. I have always stood in awe of Kenyan comrades and activists for their genius in organizing grass-root movements in adverse circumstances. Whereas their Tanzanian counterparts have prided themselves on their theoretical clarity and ideological polemics, and Ugandans have boasted of their capacity to 'take to the bush', Kenyan progressives have quietly applied their radical genius to organizing among the working people, often at a great cost to their lives and livelihoods.

## SOCIAL JUSTICE CENTERS

The Organic Intellectuals Network is a child of the mushrooming growth of social justice centers in Kenya. Beginning modestly as it did in Mathare, social justice centers now dot much of the country. Social Justice Centers take up a spectrum of varied activities and causes such as extra-judicial killings in slums and working people neighbourhoods; women's oppression; domestic violence; the plight of evicted tenants; shelter for pavement dwellers; children's rights; freedom from pollution and right to land, water and clean environment. The Social Justice Centers distinguish themselves from the normal run of NGOs in three major ways. First, their advocacy and struggles are firmly rooted in the cause of social justice for the dispossessed and the wretched. Secondly, they meticulously avoid sectarianism and puritanism without compromising their basic tenets woven around social justice. Thirdly, they do not shy away from allying with individual progressive lawyers and NGOs on particular issues and for a defined activity like a court case. While not wishing to romanticize, I can perhaps say with some certitude that Social Justice Centers serve as a school of practical struggles of the working people and their intellectuals.

## REFLECTIONS

The essays in this book draw some remarkable lessons from *Silences*, which perhaps the author could not have imagined. First, the essays situate the reflections on the book in the concrete struggles within their own organizations and movements. So the reflections are not abstract and intellectualist. Intellectualist acrobats and petty-bourgeois "buts" and "ifs" and "whereas's" are far from the thought of our activist-authors. Secondly, unlike activist scholars and intellectuals, the activist-authors of these essays do not shy away from naming imperialism while consistently appreciating that underlying neoliberalism is the barbarous system of capitalism. Neoliberalism is not a system apart from capitalism but a manifestation of capitalism in the period of all-round crisis of the system. The capitalist system's barbarity lies in the historical march of capital strewn with massive destruction of human beings and ecology and its contemporary reproduction, which gave us numerous wars, including the two world wars and possibly a third one in the making. Thirdly, while probably not articulating it as such, I see the authors are aware of the difference between reformist and revolutionary reforms. It is in this context that they characterize NGO struggles as a struggle for reforms that reinforce the system rather than lead to its revolutionary overthrow. Thus, they warn against the ever-looming danger of NGOization of social movements like theirs and derailing their agenda of revolutionary reforms by substituting reformist reform. Anyone who has worked in and with NGOs knows how the NGO discourse is subtly, gradually, but surely be adept at draining the revolutionary content of social struggles. If there ever was a neoliberal mole in revolutionary organizations, it is the NGO.

## GENESIS OF *THE SILENCES*

My intellectual encounter with the world of NGOs was when I researched my book *The Concept of Human Rights in Africa* (1989). When the book first came out, the established human rights industry captains did not notice this upstart. One such captain was personally offended, while another celebrated book reviewer thought it was demagogic and CODESRIA might want to reconsider its decision to publish it. It was in *The Concept* that I first classified and characterized NGOs. Prominent among the NGOs active in human rights at the time were INGOs (International NGOs) like Human Rights Watch and Amnesty International, most were FFUNGOs (Foreign Funded NGOs), and increasingly, we had begun to witness the rise of GONGOs (Government Organised NGOs) which were already prominent in South East Asia. Filipino comrades called them GRINGOS, American funded as they were. Funded by both the "classical" Foundations like FORD and ROCKEFELLER, I warned of the dangers of donor-dependency and NGOization of the liberation and emancipatory struggles of the working people.

At the time of writing The Concept, the Open Society Foundations (OSFs) of George Soros were not quite prominent and active in Africa. Starting in 1984, OSFs quickly penetrated the so-called dissident voices in Eastern Europe, then moved into China and the Soviet Union with the fall of the Berlin wall in 1989. They did not survive in China but managed to cause havoc in Eastern Europe and the Soviet Union. Open Society Initiatives (OSIs) moved to Africa, starting in Southern Africa in 1997, West Africa in 2000 and Eastern Africa in 2005, with their head office in Nairobi, Kenya. Soros and OSIs are clearly supportive of neoliberal economic agendas, yet using the liberal language of human rights, democracy and civil society, they manage to win over even radical elements in society.[1]

When I was writing *The Concept* the NGO world was still somewhat new in Africa. Coinciding with the consolidation of the infamous structural adjustment programs (SAPs), the situation changed rapidly, beginning in the 1990s and 2000s when various NGOs were established. Lavishly funded by imperialist governments and their foundations, all of whom were motivated by the rising neoliberal ideology of getting the state out of the economy, NGOs substituted for the people and people's organizations, including representative parliaments in policy-making bodies. The irony of governments funding non-governmental organizations apparently passed over the heads of African elites receiving the funds. The other irony was that as the neoliberal policies demanded slimming of the public service, the forcibly retired civil servants moved to NGOs, a kind of revolving door situation where former government functionaries would enter NGOs and former NGO functionaries, with no constituency or accountability of their own would play a prominent role in government policy-making bodies at the behest of funders.

## NGO PEDAGOGY

In my *Silences,* I drew the attention of the silences on many vital issues in the NGO discourse. The first silence was on the continued presence and role of imperialism in Africa. This omission was understandable. 'You do not bite the hand that feeds you', it is said. And what was the 'hand' that fed NGO elites? Of course, imperialist states and their foundations. The NGO discourse's second feature was rabid anathema to theory and history. This is well captured by some NGO slogans like 'act, don't waste time on armchair theorizing.' In many NGO meetings I have attended, I invariably come across the peculiarly NGO pedagogy located in the present paying little attention to history. The flip-chart or power-point presentations are full of charts and matrices. Any mention of history is at best tolerated, and at worse, the contributor is politely told to shut up because history is

---

[1] The chronology is taken from Open Society's own website https://www.opensocietyfoundations.org/who-we-are/our-history. Accessed 26/01/2023

ISSA G. SHIVJI

past. In many of these meetings, lead presenters on policy-making and action programs are usually activists from the global North, from whence the funds are derived. It is frustrating to see African delegates keeping mum even when a fellow odd African raises pertinent issues of history and the unequal world order dominated by imperialism. In the corridors and one-to-one conversations, these same delegates support radical interventions, but they change their position as soon as they are in the presence of the 'hand' that feeds them. Having experienced such situations, I found the essays in this volume very refreshing. They give hope that all is not lost and that there is a serious reflection on where we are coming from, where we are at and where we want to go.

## ORGANISING FOR COUNTER-HEGEMONY

Finally, one persistent question is how we organize and what form of organization would advance the cause of the working people while providing a platform for building anti-hegemonic discourses leading to counter-hegemony. While we rightly repeat with the late Tajuddin Abdulrahman, 'organize, don't agonize', we are fully justified in agonizing over the type of organization, other than NGOs, we should build, as do the contributors in this volume. This is a question of the concrete situation, and there is no textbook answer. And here, while we can learn from history and other people's struggles, our own practice is the best teacher. This is where I admire the ingenuity of our Kenyan comrades in founding a network of Social Justice Centers. My hope is that given practical struggles and experiences, our Kenyan comrades will move from a Network of Social Justice Centers to a Federation of such centers just as we have to thread together pockets of struggles into a grand coalition/federation of struggles.

On that note, I urge other East African activists to learn from the Kenyan example and think and work toward an East African Federation of Social Justice Centers.

Issa G. Shivji
Dar es Salaam
26/01/2023

# 1

# Introduction:
# Silences in the NGO Discourse

## Nicholas Mwangi & Lewis Maghanga

Since their rise to prominence in the post-Cold War period, Non-Governmental Organizations have grown exponentially in size and influence. This growth has occurred most notably under the New Policy Agenda, with Western donor states emphasizing the role of NGOs in democratization and service provision.

Through NGOs, donors have gained the power to set the development agenda for most governments, with NGOs slowly becoming Trojan horses for global neoliberalism.[1] Africa and the Global South experience the obstructive consequences of neoliberalism. The aggressive policies of the open market, privatization, and marketization of public services such as energy, water, education, health, and land have left most people in despair and hopelessness. With rising inequality and a massive economic crisis as the state transformed from a provider of public welfare into a promoter of markets, NGOs stepped in to offer solutions in the form of policies and recommendations. In the last 30 years, NGOs in Kenya and Africa, in general, have gained prominence and now play a crucial role in policymaking. In the 1980s, the fight against dictatorship and the push for multi-party democracy saw the emergence of NGOs in Kenya as civil society organizations. Their accountability, good governance, health, food, water and education programs offered hope to the oppressed. However, NGOs have not been able to solve these problems because their efforts are not adequately tied to the aspirations and struggles of grassroots communities.

The late 90s saw a good number of radicals from the social movements and left organizations joining the Civil Society and the NGO world. As James Petras put it:

> NGOs worldwide became the vehicle for upward mobility for the ambitious, educated classes; academics, journalists, and

---

[1] Wright. Glen. W. (2012). NGOs and Western hegemony: causes for concern and ideas for change. *Development in Practice, Volume 22, Number 1.* file:///C:/Users/user/Downloads/09614524.2012.634230.pdf

professionals who abandoned earlier excursions in the poorly
rewarded leftists movements for a lucrative career managing an
NGO, bringing with them their organizational and rhetorical skills
as well as a certain populist vocabulary.'[2]

As the 2022 elections in Kenya indicate, those tied to progressive
politics are meshed up with civil society and NGOs. The phenomenon
is confusing and curtails the efforts of social movements in the fight
against oppression and inequality; furthermore, their agenda becomes
obscured.

There is a tendency for social movements to die out. In the last ten
years, there has been a resurgence of social movements in Kenya. But,
one by one, many of them have disintegrated into fragments or have
dissipated completely. There are numerous reasons why social
movements don't survive that long to achieve their noble aspirations.
Opportunism, ideological bankruptcy and poor accountability are
some of the reasons that lead to the fall of social movements.
However, a more significant contributor to this downfall is the
question of NGOs and donor funding. This has plagued every
movement wherever it emerges globally, whether in Africa, Asia or
South America. This is also a matter not critically discussed here in
Kenya; studies critical of NGOs are not readily available. Progressives
have hardly documented their experiences over the last 30 years.
After the establishment of multipartyism in 1992, there was a vacuum
in the documentation of the history of the political struggles in the
country and the role of NGOs. The Organic Intellectuals Network has
thus emerged as a network of writers engaged in analyzing the socioeconomic and political situation in Kenya and Africa more generally
and documenting our history.

## NGO OPERATIONS IN KENYA

The NGO Council of Kenya website indicates that it has a membership
of over 12,000 registered organizations comprising international,
regional, and local NGOs. There are numerous NGOs in Kenya
operating in various areas, such as informal urban settlements and
rural areas and are involved in different issues such as health,
education, advocacy, environmental conservation, children and
women's rights and gender-based violence. However, only 4 percent
of NGOs in Kenya are primarily interested in governance issues such
as democracy, human rights and corruption.

In Kenya's urban centers, the informal settlements of Kibera and
Mathare, located within Nairobi city county, host the highest number

---

[2] Petras, John. (1999) NGOs: In the service of imperialism, Journal
of Contemporary Asia, 29:4, 429-440, DOI: 10.1080/00472339980000221

of NGOs, being the largest and second-largest slums in Kenya, respectively. Within Kenya's informal settlements, poverty, unemployment, inadequate health facilities, lack of education, and poor sanitation inhibit attaining a decent and dignified life. Most organizations based in these areas are involved in such issues in one way or another. Most international NGOs in Kenya have origins in Western Europe and North America, where most of those founded locally also draw their funding.

## WHY THIS BOOK?

Members of the Organic Intellectuals Network are active organizers in the struggle to achieve social justice. They have experienced the contradictions of the NGO discourse and, just like others before them, have found themselves in the struggle versus survival dilemma. To get a clear picture of our contemporary struggles and the despair of NGOs operating in the proletarian movement, comrades decided to reflect, study, and analyze Prof. Issa Shivji's book *Silences in NGO Discourse: The Role and Future of NGOs in Africa*. For the authors, these analyses and reflections are based on personal experiences in their day-to-day organizing.

In summarizing the authors' observations regarding the impacts of NGOs in organizing, this book calls into question the fundamental question, 'why do NGOs exist?' To answer this question, the authors provide a historical chronology of the resistance in Kenya, Zimbabwe and the rest of Africa, relating those to the subjective factors at every period. Through this, a scientific relationship can be drawn between social movements and NGOs in our current epoch.

From their experiences with NGOs, the authors, representing grassroots social movements, highlight the dangers associated with donor funding. Often, donor funding ends abruptly after making people dependent on them, creating severe strain on grassroots organizations. The more one engages with NGOs, the softer one becomes to critique NGOs, particularly in highlighting their relationship to imperialism. Further, NGOs usually help in driving reforms. However, they play no part in revolutionary work.

As a result, they merely preserve the present order and help exacerbate the frustrations arising from massive inequality in our society. In the long run, NGOs play a critical role in stifling the development and independence of grassroots social movements.

# 2

# Nothing Going On: Mobilization as a Tool of Demobilization

## Sungu Oyoo

Prof. Issa Shivji has remained true to the Pan- Africanist cause over the years. His thoughts, ideas, and analyses have retained unparalleled freshness and continued resonance across generations. Likewise, his poignant critiques have remained relevant, like in the late 1960s or early 1970s when he wrote Tanzania: The Silent Class Struggle. So when I heard from Comrades Lewis Maghanga and Nicholas Mwangi that Shivji's paper, Silences in the NGO Discourse, would be the subject of our latest round of reflections, I knew that I should read it, reflect on it and write some thoughts about it.

In Silences in the NGO Discourse, Shivji firmly asserts that the role of NGOs in Africa cannot be understood without a precise characterization of the current historical moment. He examines the national project and its impediments, taking us back to the partition of Africa before examining the colonial legacy. He then proceeds to examine the nationalist challenge and the defeat of the national (Pan-African) project; Pan-Africanism vs. territorial nationalism; the developmental state vs. democratic development; and nationalism vs. imperialism. Shivji concludes this historical journey by looking at the imperial project and its succors, including the neoliberal offensive.

Beyond this critical framework, Shivji 'depicts Africa at the crossroads of the defeat of the national project and the rehabilitation of the imperial project', constantly reminding us that 'in the neoliberal offensive, the roles of NGOs are economic, political and ideological'. Capitalism and imperialism have taken different forms of camouflage in different historical epochs – from slavery to colonialism, neo-colonialism, and the neoliberal world order that today ravages, exploits, dehumanizes, and humiliates Africans and countless peoples and territories across the world. Shivji reminds us that:

The national liberation struggles of the 1960s and 1970s, which put imperialism on the ideological defensive, have been aborted ... Imperialism by the name of globalization is returning while refurbishing its moral and ideological image ... NGOs were born in the womb of neoliberalism and knowingly or otherwise are participating in the imperial project.

As I read the last paragraphs of Prof. Shivji's paper, I could not help but connect parallels between the NGO-industrial complex and what we should perhaps refer to as the movement-building industrial complex. My reflections below are thus not an attempt to reiterate Shivji's brilliant ideas but to analyze the movement landscape in parts of Africa and how that movement landscape replicates the silences in NGO discourse - knowingly or unwittingly.

## THE MOVEMENT BUILDING INDUSTRIAL COMPLEX

After a decade where movements have, once again, been at the forefront of change on many territories across the African continent, we find ourselves in an epoch where 'movement-building support' has become another buzzword in NGO circles. NGOs jostle over which movements to 'support' and allocate millions of dollars annually toward this. A good proportion of these dollars come from foundations and other proxies interested in limiting how radical the organizing trajectory of movements can be, thereby shaping the nature of people's struggles.

That is not to say that NGOs have an infinite influence on the activities, organizing and political trajectory of all movements. Exceptions, as Shivji asserts, exist.

> Once in the donor trap, movements find the parameters of their organizing defined through log frames, outcomes, outputs, and whatever other words or trends may be in vogue. Many NGOs focus on a particular issue for a limited period before moving on to 'the next big thing'. And just like in the NGO world where 'focus on donor funding determines demands', some movements shift their areas of focus every few years in line with donor funding. Over time, these movements, just like the NGOs they are replicating, have worked on some issues without sufficiently tackling any single problem – and 'communities are again left grappling'. In this theatre, 'issue-oriented' movements are encouraged. In contrast, cohesive mass movements capable of analyzing the issues and their underlying basis are referred to as radical and locked out of their spaces.

Many young people who genuinely wish to see a better world and who join these movements - whether they regard themselves as activists, organizers or community leaders - are tunneled into a framework of organizing that discourages theory, either explicitly or implicitly. Shivji states, 'The requirements of funding agencies subtly discourage, if not exhibiting outright hostility to a historical, social and theoretical understanding of development, poverty and discrimination.'

But why would our movements attempt to struggle without a 'concrete analysis of the concrete situation'? Shivji reminds us that unlike the 60s and 70s when 'radical intellectual activism was integrated with militant activism', we are in an epoch where 'theory is eschewed and activism privileged' by design.

## YOU CANNOT BOX PEOPLE'S STRUGGLES INTO LOG FRAMES

Shivji writes:

> The inherent bias against theory is manifested at various levels. I will mention a couple. First, the penchant for project funding, which is supposed to be operated and completed within a given time - a triennium for example - does not admit thinking about the underlying premises of the so-called project. The managerial techniques of monitoring and evaluating projects through log-frames by their very nature compartmentalize and dissect life to such an extent that the sight of the whole, even the capacity to think holistically, is lost. Secondly, the projects are issue-based and are supposed to be addressed as issues. The issue itself is identified as a problem at the level of phenomenon; its underlying basis is not addressed but assumed. The issue is isolated and abstracted from its social, economic and historical reality; therefore, its interconnectedness to other issues and the whole is lost ... Theory, and particularly grand theory, is dismissed as academicism, unworthy of activists. Yet, we know, that every practice gives rise to theory and that every action is based on some theoretical or philosophical premise or outlook. NGO action is also based on certain theoretical premises and philosophical outlooks.

The negative attitude of donors towards critical analysis is firmly integrated into NGOs that play the role of the donor to our movements. This attitude is replicated within some movements - especially those whose leadership and organizing need to be grounded in theory and political education that reinforces political awareness of the terrain within which these movements exist and operate. Within such movements, cadres engaging in critical analyses are often ridiculed or dismissed as 'show-offs' or wasomi. In this predicament, backward elements within the movements push them toward the all-too-familiar path of donor theory and log frames. From time to time, words like revolution, freedom, class struggle and Pan-Africanism are often thrown into this pot to create confusion every once in a while. Such movements embody organized chaos, the dance to nowhere that today characterizes the African revolution.

Fortunately, some movements and organizations across the continent have established political education cells and brigades. Here in Kenya, the Revolutionary Socialist League, the Social Justice Movement, Kongamano la Mapinduzi, and the Communist Party of Kenya, among others, readily come to mind in this regard. At the same time, platforms like Ukombozi Library, Cheche Bookshop and Comrades Bookstore continue to provide avenues that enable access to information, texts and discourse that aid in political education.

Political education and the theory it exposes cadres within our movements enables us to understand the interconnected nature of the neoliberal system acting in the interest of global imperialism. It allows us to define strategies for combatting local agents of capital and their masters across the oceans. Understanding this system lets us realize that we cannot silo our struggles. Our local actions need to be connected to a collective outlook and shared frames of organizing around radical African feminism, political liberation, economic emancipation, ecological justice and a Pan-African re-calibration.

As Shivji states,

> Taking for granted the fundamentals of neoliberalism and financial capitalism, or challenging them only piecemeal on specific issues, for example debt, environment or gender discrimination, actually draws the NGOs as protagonists into the imperial project.

Given the conditions of our people within the capitalist-imperialist system, African movements cannot afford to be drawn as protagonists in the imperial project. These movements must continually strive to transform into mass-based movements capable of making things move. It is not a movement if it is not moving people, events or processes.

## MOBILIZATION AS A TOOL OF DE-MOBILIZATION

Shivji writes:

> NGOs are led by and largely composed of the educated elite. They are located in urban areas and well-versed in the language and idiom of modernization ... Broadly, three types of NGO elites may be identified. The first category is the radical elite that was previously involved in political struggles, with an explicit vision for change and transformation. However, it found itself suppressed under the statist hegemony. As a result, many of these elites took the opportunity to express themselves politically in the NGOs. They saw NGOs as a possible terrain of struggle for change ... The second category includes well-intentioned individuals driven by altruistic motives to improve the conditions of their fellow human beings and compatriots. In other words, they are morally motivated ... The third category is the mainstream elite, not infrequently former government bureaucrats, who shifted to the NGO world once they found that donor funding was being directed there. The motivation of this elite is simply careerist.

There is no greater tragedy than when the oppressed adopt the image of their oppressor. Over time, individuals and factions within the movement dismantle previously existing horizontal leadership to enable them to emerge as leaders. Another individual, seeing a pathway to treasures, declares themselves treasurer. Others scheme on how to siphon the donor dollars from the movement. But still, some continue organizing along the political lines that initially brought all together. The movement degenerates. As elections approach, individuals within some of these movements align with right-wing and reactionary political parties. For that is what butters their bread and pays their rent. Movement work and movement-building, by this stage, have become a full-blown economic activity camouflaged in slogans. Anything and anyone that stands in the way of these slogans is pushed aside, ridiculed, humiliated, intimidated, suspended, or eventually expelled from the movement.

But why this?

The three types of elites described by Prof. Shivji above are identifiable within our movements.

First, there are those individuals who 'have a clear vision for change and transformation, and having been actively involved in struggles in years gone by' and are today actively mentoring cadres within various movements. Some of them, well in their senior years, are still dedicating time and energy to breathing life into people's struggles for justice and dignity. Others are increasingly involved in political and electoral organizing on arriving at a realization that the problems we are organizing against need political solutions. But, unfortunately, over the decades, some people in this category have evolved into opportunists, unrecognizable even among people they formerly called 'comrade'.

Then there's a second category that comprises those who join movements with the best intentions, driven by altruistic motives. This category includes allies and potential comrades within the movement. Like transistor radios, they need tuning through patient conversation and political education. Many younger cadres in our movements fall into this category. More importantly, this category also comprises those constantly struggling to keep the movement along a correct political line. They frequently organize, ground with brothers and sisters, and engage in political education, self-reflection, and self-criticism. Their theory informs their practice, and their practice their theory. They are the rocks that anchor the movement.

The third category, which Shivji refers to as 'the mainstream elite', is also replicated in our movements. They exist in various shapes and sizes. Many have careerist motivation, and they view the movements as a pedestal that can help them achieve greater ambitions- political, economic or otherwise – in the present or later. Then there's the cocktail of counter-revolutionaries. And the state agents.

Individuals within the different categories jostle for the position of spokesman to get recognition in the eyes of the people, the media, and the NGOs with economic leverage. Under these circumstances, mobilization becomes a tool for de-mobilization. Fragmented and weakened, the organization becomes a tool for disorganization.

Professor Issa Shivji's paper, Silences in the NGO Discourse, is a must-read for all African people who wish to understand the role NGOs play in the political economy of Africa and the rest of the third world by extension. Its publication over a decade ago was timely, and its clarity today is timeless.

# 3

# The Struggle of Movement Building Against NGOization in Kenya[1]

## Kinuthia Ndungu

In his poem 'Remember', Ndungi Githuku says, 'We got to see where we are coming from, so as to see where we are going to...' Prof Issa Shivji, in *Silences in the NGO Discourse*, has applied scientific analysis to highlight the ideological, economic, and political role of NGOs in expanding and consolidating neoliberal hegemony in the global context. He has shown that poverty is not a product of nature but created through a historical process of exploitation and neoliberalism built upon and impacted by the legacy of colonialism. This rich analysis is relevant to those of us organizing within social movements. NGOs have a history of infiltrating, diluting, subverting, and destroying mass movements. Our country inherited and has maintained the colonial state since the 1920s. In 1963, we had a false start. The freedom fighters lost it to the opportunistic loyalist camp of Jomo Kenyatta that kept the colonial state intact. The structure of the neo-colonial state has not disappeared.

Prof Shivji locates the rise of NGOs in the neoliberal insurgency of 1980-90. In 1981 the World Bank published the report, 'Accelerated Development for Africa: an Agenda for Africa'. The report and its subsequent Structural Adjustment Programmes focused on stabilization measures. As Prof Shivji Aawas the neoliberal ideological offensive: the period when the policy of marketization, privatization and liberalization, or the logic of plunder, was imposed on the African states. In Kenya, this was the decade of massive retrenchments of public employees. It was when sugar factories in Nyanza and Western regions, textile industries in the Rift Valley, and government-supported milk processing plants like the Kenya Cooperative Creameries (KCC) collapsed as these and other national assets were privatized. It was also when small farming cooperatives shut down as agricultural extension services and farming subsidies were

[1] This essay is dedicated to the memory of Comrade Alphonse Ngenga of Githurai Social Justice Centre and Young Communist League. A 21-year-old victim of the government's neoliberal market-based approach to public healthcare.

withdrawn, forcing people to relocate from the rural to the informal urban settlements in search of employment. It was the epoch of the decline of social services like healthcare and education and a rise in corruption, crime, and an upsurge of street families, an era of greater yet illusory freedoms. This was when we walked into a valley of confusion about democracy and the multi-party system.

As states focused on implementing neoliberalism's extractive, inhumane logic, they surrendered their traditional role. Bilateral and multilateral institutions set aside significant funds to mitigate the massive devastation caused by these economic policies. As a result, there was a rise in NGOs funded by and relying almost exclusively on foreign funding. They were filling the vacuum created by the retreating state. This marked the return of imperialism while refurbishing its moral and ideological image. They became the new missionaries on the continent. We reminisce about 2002 when many NGOs vehemently opposed President Kibaki's free education program because they were getting funding in the guise of educating the poor. To NGOs, poverty is the goose that lays golden eggs.

From the examination in the book, colonial and imperial history remains at the heart of our current condition. We are stuck with neoliberal policies that our oppressors praise. We have a historical obligation to free ourselves from economic slavery. However, it is crystal clear that NGOs are not in a position to either expose or oppose imperial domination as they work for the interest of global imperialism. Their agenda is determined by the bilateral and multilateral institutions and the western governments that bankroll them. We certainly don't expect them to bite the hands that feed them — 'whoever pays the piper plays the tune'.

Today, about 40 Social Justice Centers across the country inspire the human rights movement from a social justice perspective starting from the bottom of society. The centers are networked through the Social Justice Centers Working Group (SJCWG), which comprises two representatives from each center. It also acts as the secretariat for the Social Justice Centers in Kenya, a movement inspired by the ideas of Pan–Africanism trying to organize and mobilize communities in the informal settlements around social justice issues. The Social Justice Centers have organized various successful campaigns against police brutality and demands for social justice. For the 5th year in a row, SJCWG organized the annual Saba Saba March for Our Lives, commemorating and building on the pro-democracy struggles of the early 1990s. Over 1500 people, mostly youth and women, marched from their communities in a march dubbed Njaa Revolution (Hunger Revolution), protesting the high cost of living, enduring police brutality, and increased public debt levels, among other concerns. The success of the Social Justice Movement has led to sizeable civil society organizations with close to no ties with the poor population in the informal settlements, but with donor resources coming knocking to work with the movement.

Amilcar Cabral reminds us to learn from life, learn from our people, learn from books, learn from the experience of others, and never stop learning. Prof Shivji's book challenges the Organic Intellectuals Network to learn from the current struggles of the people and creatively appropriate intellectual insights on the role of NGOs in their political and historical context. This will allow them to offer direction as a vanguard to the movement.

The Release Political Prisoners (RPP) movement offers excellent lessons to our social movement. Between 1991-1997, RPP managed to hold workshops for community awareness and mobilization through personal donations and the commitment of its members and well-wishers. Their successes attracted the interest of international donor organizations. In 1997, they opened their doors to donor partnerships. This ushered in internal contradictions within the movement. The funds were accompanied by conditions on how they would conduct their activities; they were now tied by the donor programs. Credentialism was introduced. Professionalizing the movement favored those with academic or other formal qualifications, while those who had their education curtailed due to political and economic reasons were left to languish in poverty. As a result, the agendas of the movement were hijacked. They were detached from the grassroots social force of the workers and peasants and captured by the academia and the intelligentsia.

Kenya's mainstream human rights organizations that partner with international donors and western embassies engage professional consultants to conduct background assessments and develop strategic plans for social movements. Like the tactics employed against RPP, this is aimed at controlling and sabotaging the formation of formidable radical social and political forces from the grassroots. The book is clear that one of the aims of these donor NGOs operating under the guise of human rights and freedom is to diffuse political anger and blunt the edges of political resistance. The Organic Intellectuals Network must, through persuasion and constant debates, endeavor to open the eyes of the movement membership to the impracticability of building the movement under such terms of engagement.

Bunge La Mwananchi (The Peoples Parliament) movement, which emerged as an organic grassroots social movement and revolutionized grassroots politics in Kenya in the era of neoliberal globalization in the early 1990s, is today a shadow of its former self. This is because Bunge was infiltrated and undermined by neoliberal NGOs threatened by an organized grassroots social movement. The NGOs capitalized on most Bunge members' poor material conditions (as many were unemployed) to turn them into 'guns for hire' who would mobilize and join their activities and demonstrations, whatever the cause, at a fee (transport reimbursement, facilitation fees, etc.). This created a culture of dependency on handouts, making it challenging to coordinate movement activities without money. The Social Justice Movement is grappling with a similar challenge as its morally motivated cadres and community members are in the bleakness of the struggle for livelihoods and, therefore, vulnerable to the commodification of resistance.

Bunge La Mwananchi is today run by opportunists and ideologically bankrupt individuals, sycophants of bankrupt politicians who are life members of pro-capitalist political parties. The NGOs are less interested in their activities than before because they offer no real threat to the neoliberal establishment. However, the degeneration of Bunge provides invaluable lessons for our movement. The advances made by these NGOs eventually led to the corruption of its members. They ultimately lose sight of the movement's goals, resulting in disorganization and depoliticization.

We recognize that the relationship between the movement and progressive NGOs has helped the members (grassroots human rights defenders) continue advancing the struggle for social change. They have sponsored training for members in diverse fields relevant to their work as human rights defenders, such as the training of paralegals. They have also continuously offered solidarity whenever members are intimidated, arbitrarily arrested, or facing malicious charges in defense of human rights and social justice. The partnerships have also made a number of the movement's activities successful. However, Shivji has highlighted that these NGOs have historical and ideological limitations in advancing our struggle for social change. They are funded by the same agents of neoliberalism and austerity that trigger social movements. Therefore, our relationship and interaction should remain tactical.

Notably, the struggle for social justice must guarantee the people's material needs, such as food security, decent housing, free education, and free healthcare is a political struggle. It is a struggle against the dehumanizing legacy of a neoliberal capitalist economy whose guiding ideology is hate for the poor and greed for profit. We, therefore, need ideological clarity to widen the movement's base to form a political and social force. We must form alliances with progressive political parties and social movements to have a united front that will champion social change and alternative political leadership in the country.

Additionally, we must learn from the generations previously involved in political struggles in the country. After the triumph of the progressive forces in the 2002 general elections, a majority were co-opted by the NGOs. As a result, most lost touch with the makers of history and were either silent or writing and giving lectures and interviews on how to make revolutions or about their experiences in the Nyayo and Nyati House torture chambers.

The late Comrade Onyango Oloo reminds us of the necessity to restore the ideological foundation of the Kenyan Social Movement. Let us resist the urge to NGOize our movement. But, there shall be a price to pay.

A luta continua!

# 4

# A Reflection on
# *Silences in the NGO Discourse*

## Lewis Maghanga

An analysis of the objective and subjective conditions for revolutionary change would reveal that certain factors act as catalysts for progress while others work as inhibitors. In our constant organizing, it is paramount that we remain scientific in our approach and that we constantly analyze phenomena and everything around us dialectically. That means we must inquire objectively into any given scenario, considering its pros and cons and making concrete deductions from whatever we have observed. In our case, as we keep organizing towards revolutionary change, we are compelled to look into our organizations as well as into the general revolutionary situation of the country by analyzing our strengths, weaknesses, opportunities, and threats, as well as constantly evaluating our goals and progress. This is the essence of being scientific in our approach to organizing.

This reflection on *Silences in the NGO Discourse* seeks to pay attention to the role played by NGOs in the ever-spinning wheel of societal development and what their impact has been on the general progress of our society. Issa Shivji's paper critically examines the role and future of NGOs in Africa in the light of their self-perception as non-governmental, non-political, non-partisan, non-ideological, non-academic, non-theoretical, non-profit associations of well-intentioned individuals dedicated to changing the world to make it a better place for the poor, marginalized and downcast. The paper argues that the role of NGOs in Africa cannot be understood without a precise characterization of the current historical moment. 'I do not doubt the noble motivations and good intentions of NGO leaders and activists. But we do not judge a process's outcome by its authors' intentions. We aim to analyze the objective effects of actions, regardless of their intentions.'

## REFLECTIONS

I locate the rise, prominence, and privileging of the NGO sector in the womb of the neoliberal offensive. Its aims are ideological, economic, and political. NGO discourse, or, more correctly, non-discourse, is predicated on the philosophical and political premises of the neoliberal or globalization paradigm.

Indeed, one cannot separate the development of the NGOs from the onset of the Structural Adjustment Programmes, the remodeling of the global economy to facilitate proper domination of the working class by the capitalist class, and the rampant and unrestricted exploitation of the world's resources by the capitalist system. However, it would be wrong to present the relationship between Western NGOs and official aid agencies in the 1980s as the product of some conscious conspiracy, as with colonial missionary organizations. On the contrary, the co-option of NGOs into the neoliberal cause reflects a coincidence in ideologies rather than a purposeful plan. The proponents of neoliberalism saw in charitable development the possibility of enforcing the unjust social order they desired by consensual rather than coercive means — an excellent merger of interests and an opportunity for masking the intention and nature of the capitalist system.

The Capitalist system thrives on the notion of 'hard work', 'enterprise' and 'free will'. It seeks to present the appropriation of wealth as the product of a legitimate systematic arrangement and smart calculation. This is intended to legitimize it as the best mode of production. This sought-after legitimacy aims to generate as little resistance as possible and facilitate unhindered exploitation of the world's resources and labor. 'Success' is made to appear as the by-product of chance, not exploitation.

Wherein, though, lies the source of this kind of thinking?

A good look into the world outlook of the dominant capitalist class would reveal idealism as the philosophy used to view society, nature and, indeed, all phenomena. But what does this mean?

This means that, in the lens of the ruling class, the world's origin is a mystery and is outside and unconnected with our daily life and experiences. It is impossible to fully understand the world, as some aspects of the universe are unknowable. Further, those phenomena in the natural world are not inter-connected; one natural occurrence is isolated from other such events in the natural environment. That history develops as a straight line, not as a product of constant antagonism between the various classes and modes of production that have existed, and that historical events are the products of the 'brave' work of 'outstanding' individuals and an 'agglomeration of accidents', not the collective work of the members of the society. Finally, for the universe to thrive, we must constantly hope for the 'charitable' work of the 'mysterious originator' of the world.

The effect of this world outlook is that it leads to a top-down mentality in the approach to any phenomenon. Solving any problems society faces takes the 'charitable work' of outstanding individuals and organizations. Voila – the appearance and need for NGOs.

This kind of thinking can be contrasted with the materialist conception of phenomena, which places human society at the center of its actions and never divorces human beings from their role as facilitators of their historical development. Materialism places primacy on nature and matter as what influences historical development. Materialism holds that historical development is the product of a constant struggle between classes and modes of production.

The Shivji also touches on the globalization offensive as going hand in hand with the neoliberal agenda and the development of NGOs. With neoliberalAat, national liberation ideologies have been rubbished, and national self-determination declared passé. Africa is told it has only one choice: integrate fully into the globalized world, or remain marginalized. The specter of marginalization is so rampant that even progressive African scholars dare say that 'Africa may be graduating from being the region with "lost development decades" to becoming the world's forgotten continent' (Mkandawire & Soludo). The former US ambassador to Tanzania, blatant about what the superpower expected of African states, is quoted as, "The liberation diplomacy of the past when alliances with socialist nations were paramount, and so-called Third World Solidarity dominated foreign policy, must give way to a more realistic approach to dealing with your true friends – those who are working to lift you into the twenty-first century, where poverty is not acceptable, and disease must be conquered." African leaders are left with little option: 'you are either with globalization or doomed!'

The author makes critique of the notion that NGOs are in fact, non-political. Politics is concerned with the distribution of resources, and one cannot, therefore, divorce political questions from economic questions. Indeed, those who command production wield power; the ruling class in every epoch of history are those in control of the means of production.

In summary, therefore, the author outlines the following concepts as the silences in the NGO discourse:

1. What NGOs actually are. Arising out of the neoliberal and globalization agenda, they appear as elitist and intimately connected to the imperialist world, where they actually draw their funding. They are thus not in service of the community but of their donors.
2. A seeking to change the world without actually understanding it; this is because of the idealist world outlook that dominates the thinking of the ruling class. Clearly, communities are hardly involved in policymaking, and the approach is usually top-down.
3. An acceptance of the permanent present, not looking into the historical origins of the world's problems today.

4. Looking at society as a harmonious whole of stakeholders driven by a desire to deny the existence of the class struggle between the exploiters and the exploited in a bid to conceal exploitation itself. Social welfare and the provision of basic needs and services to the community are no longer the responsibility of the state or the private sector; instead, they are assigned to NGOs. Thus the 'holy trinity' of development partners is completed: state, capital and NGOs, the latter supposedly the major stakeholders in the participatory development enterprise. The net effect legitimizes the exploitative capitalist system presented as pro-poor and morally driven by the so-called NGO sector.

5. A presentation of non-governmental as non-political, thereby attempting to separate politics and economics, state and civil society, in the interests of the bourgeoisie.

NGOs were born in the womb of neoliberalism and knowingly or otherwise are participating in the imperial project. And rightly so.

# 5

# Pan-Africanism and the NGO Discourse

## Wanjira Wanjiru

*The present cannot fully be understood and grasped, nor the future charted without constantly keeping in the forefront of our minds the century-old process cited by Walter Rodney on How Europe Underdeveloped Africa.*

In this book, Prof. Issa Shivji demonstrates how Imperialism continues to thrive and will need more than meets the eye to comprehend. The system that oppressed millions of Africans 500 years ago is still in place today.

NGOs go with definitions and principles such as non-governmental, non-political, non-partisan, non-ideological, non-academic, non-rhetorical, and a non-profit association of good people hell-bent on making the world a better place, right? But is it? Or is it holding us back from actualizing our absolute liberation as oppressed people of Africa? Shivji says he does not doubt the good intentions of NGO leaders and activists, but we must analyze the objective effects of actions regardless of their intentions.

Reading this book evoked feelings of sadness in me. On top of five centuries of slavery, we are now tied to our former colonial masters in the name of globalization and neoliberalism. The Berlin conference held in 1884 by imperialists still dictates to us, as Africans were to draw the border more than 100 years later. That the process was so successful on top of having nation-states with different colonial masters, we now have the birth of non-governmental organizations, which are indeed very governmental.

This book has deepened my understanding of the role of NGOs in Africa. More importantly, it gives a precise analysis of the genesis of NGOs. Post-independence Africa had great visionaries for the continent. An example is Gaddafi, who proposed one currency for all Africans, a radical proposal that had him assassinated. Ghana's liberation hero Kwame Nkrumah cautioned against nationalism, saying individual states would be pawns for imperialist chessboards. Sister states would be pinned against each other. This was illustrated in the Democratic Republic of Congo when western imperial powers conspired to assassinate the great Patrice Lumumba, subjecting

Congo to many wars and stealing minerals while posing as UN peacekeepers. In Kenya, there have been various incursions by the Kenyan state machinery on areas in and around Somalia since the Shifta wars in the sixties. Kenya currently maintains boots in Somalia on the pretext of national security. History has absolved Nkrumah. If only we had a unified stance as African people! We are indeed stronger together. As Mwalimu Nyerere said, 'African nationalism is meaningless. It's anachronic if it is not, at the same time, Pan-Africanism'.

With the establishment of nation-states, and Pan-Africanism taking a hit, it was fertile ground for imperialism to thrive. Structural Adjustment Programmes were introduced to the new governments, which had no choice but to comply. Pressure from the International Monetary Fund did force their hand in structuring neoliberal policies that ensured foreign actors' domination of local economies and, ultimately, dependence on financial aid. Aid that came with many strings attached. You either join the bandwagon of globalization or be isolated. Many African presidents succumbed to the pressure, and this is how we are modern-day slaves. Slaves of debts we know nothing about. Kenya National treasury CS Ukur Yatani says $ 24.4 billion of our GDP will be in the form of interest payments to the Exum Bank of China and China development bank. The interest rate on external debt jumps to a staggering $138 Billion in 2021/2022, notwithstanding. It's the same colonial system, just a few changes to the game.

NGO discourse, or more correctly, non-discourse, is predicated on the philosophical and political premises of the neoliberal paradigm-Shivji.

To bring the situation closer to home, whenever we document a case within the Social Justice Centers, we have to send data to NGOs for them to come in and salvage the situation. At Mathare Social Justice Centre, we have a caseload of files submitted to NGOs, including those that belong to the government, to enable us to get justice for victims of police excesses. Year after year, we keep adding to the file. The community barely experiences any change. It is this thinking we reject. The solution to our problems is somewhat out of our reach, and we must rely on external help that the people are incapable of solving community issues unless NGOs step in. Where is the role of the leadership elected by the people? NGOs make governments lazy. The scope of NGOs in Africa is so immense that it could also be another arm of government, with millions of dollars in funding and vague agendas. Agendas like eradication of poverty, yet poverty is rapidly increasing by the day. And we cannot begin to talk about eradication without discussing poverty's genesis. How did we find ourselves here, with such disparities between the haves and have-nots? To blind us further, they keep us dancing to their tune with the theory of human rights. When our children are exploited for their labor; women are exploited for their bodies and labor; when police kill people; when poverty, violent as it is, is the order of the day, it is nothing more than a human right issue. A humanitarian crisis at best, and we are already looking outside of ourselves for solutions. We don't scratch beyond the surface. It is not immediately apparent to us that all these things are man-made. That it is an illusion of scarcity. We, as a continent, are in absolute abundance, fully endowed with natural and human resources. But our people are wallowing in poverty in their millions, and NGOs are thriving under the pretext of fixing things.

NGOs have been putting patches on a torn dress; the dress is now way too torn. We demand a new dress. We must demand a new way of life, away from aid and charity, where society is truly egalitarian. Where being human is enough. Where dignity is a birthright, we Africans must be at the forefront of actualizing this reality. The scholars must unite with activists and forge a united front for the complete liberation of the African people. This generation of Africans must rebel. We are gracefully following in the wisdom of the Pan-Africanists before us, careful not to repeat a mistake made before.

We must unite and rebel against European-engineered borders, from Cape to Cairo, Morocco to Madagascar, one united African state. This means that sitting African presidents will have to give up their sovereignties, the armies, and their entourages. Put down their egos and give way to the people's will. We know that this is an uphill task by the nature of present-day African presidents, such as Yoweri Museveni of Uganda, Ali Bongo Ondimba of Gabon, and Paul Biya of Cameroon. A task we must undertake nonetheless.

So, strap on your seatbelts, and let us embark on this liberation journey. A bumpy ride worth all its while. Africa must be free. Africa will be free.

Our homeland or death,
We shall win.

# 6

# NGOs, Capitalism and Imperialism

## Mwaivu wa Kaluka

Non-governmental organizations came into being due to the neoliberal offensive, beginning in the late '70s and early '80s. Though Prof Shivji tracked its inception as a neoliberal offensive when civil society had become vogue in the 1980s (see page 30), I will try and illustrate why I think otherwise. He has shown explicitly how the national project failed and given outstanding historical accounts of what happened.

To fully understand the NGO discourse, it is best if we go back to the Bretton Woods conference and its offspring; the World Bank, IMF et al. that was formed after the Second World War to bail out capitalism from the ruins of war and its periodic crises that are inherent in it. This was also the transition period from monopoly capitalism which Lenin had predicted, to a new face of generalized monopoly capitalism characterized by concentration and centralization of capital within the centers (Advanced Industrialized countries) at the detriment of the periphery (developing countries).

But it was not until 1973, during the OPEC oil embargo and debt crisis in the US and Europe, that the metropole countries began to apply the instrumentality of the IMF and the World Bank. These institutions dominated economic policymaking in Africa; the structural adjustment programs were prescribed to almost all African economies. They failed miserably and wreaked havoc on our economies, leading to growing public discontent among the African people and those from the peripheries in other continents who were victims of neoliberal policies.

The US, the European Union, and countries from the center came up with a plan to cushion their imperial hegemony; they thought of this third sector (NGO) between the state and private enterprise to continue advancing their neoliberal and globalization agenda. That's why it was a defensive mechanism rather than an offensive mechanism, as proposed by Shivji. These NGOs were made up of top-down organizational structures and led by educated elites and some privileged petit-bourgeois intellectuals. One of their striking hallmarks was their opposition to statism. But on the other hand, World Bank and Western Foundations co-opted and encouraged NGOs to undermine the national welfare state by providing social services to a narrow scope of people whom the effects of multinational corporations and neoliberalism had ravaged.

Africa became a subject matter of the Poverty Reduction Strategy Papers, authored by consultants who met at stakeholders' conferences in high-end hotels instead of protracted public debates that involved the masses. The state's role of ensuring its citizens' well-being was abdicated; it was subordinated to the position of chief supervisor of the globalization project under the guidance of the imperialist powers, who called themselves development partners and true friends. Even when they talked of issues such as gender equality, climate change, environmental degradation, feminism, youth empowerment, people living with disabilities and health and nutrition issues, they only did so in a reactionary manner. They failed to look into the root cause and the possible extermination of those problems.

These NGOs only act as a bridge between the monopoly capitalists and the metropoles. They will not be able to provide long-term and sustainable solutions since they only focus on the technical and financial assistance of projects that do not touch on the whole population. Instead of looking at the structural conditions that shape our everyday life, they need to be more aware of their limitations. Therefore, they are counterrevolutionary in isolating themselves from the masses and undermining class-based solidarity organizations such as trade unions, peasant associations and the like. Moreover, they need to tackle the material economic conditions which give rise to these political and social problems.

In most cases, NGOs stress private responsibility for social problems; they see laissez-faire market economics as the alpha and omega for development with minimal intervention from the state. The writer also agrees with Karl Marx's position that the economic base is the fundamental determinant of the political and social superstructure when he shows that the separation of politics from economics is a bourgeois deception; that politics is the quintessence or concentrated form of economics. The political sphere is organized based on how people produce their means of livelihood and their relations in production, distribution, and exchange. NGOs calling themselves non-political and non-profit is, therefore, something that requires serious interrogation. Prof Shivji notes that when NGOs accept the myth of being non-political, they continue with the mystification and legitimization of the system of capitalist production. They become allies of the status quo and the project of its maintenance.

Additionally, these NGOs get funding from the imperialists, and as the adage goes, "he who pays the piper calls the tune". This means participation in any activity with these NGOs may be meaningless, which is why most of them involve a small elite clique and are not mass-based. The people at the top are accountable to and work under the direction of the donors; there needs to be more public participation. Mass opinions and deliberations do not inform the policies. On the contrary, their policy strategies are to facilitate the legitimization of neoliberal policies.

In the future, NGOs should operate among the people, learn from them, and try to change their material conditions and inspire their revolutionary spirit for change. They should move out of those stakeholder workshops where they discuss poverty reduction strategies and join the working people of Africa in their struggle against oppression. They should be critical of the creation of poverty through the concentration of the means of production in a few hands and the appropriation and subjugation of labor by the bourgeoisie and foreign capital, as well as the privatization of social services that is saddled with corruption and bloated bureaucracy. They can show solidarity with trade unions, and their attitude should be anti-capitalist and anti-imperialist if they are genuine about the struggle of the suffering people.

# 7

# Neoliberalism Won't Save Us

## Nicholas Mwangi

N eoliberalism is the root cause of all our problems. In *Silences in NGO Discourse: The Role and Future of NGOs in Africa*, Prof. Shivji points out the rise of the NGOs and their apparent role in Africa as part of the Neo-liberal and ideological offensive. NGOs are neither neutral nor non-ideological as we are meant to believe. That is not to say there are no genuine people with good intentions working with NGOs; however, as Shivji, puts it, 'Unless there is self-consciousness on their part of this fundamental moment in the struggle between imperialism & nationalism, the NGOs end up playing the role of ideological and foot soldiers of imperialism by whatever name called.'

We are at a time when we must interrogate this discourse, especially for those organizing within social resistance movements. As Arundhati Roy warns, a major hazard facing mass movements is the NGOization of resistance; this thus calls for scrutiny of this phenomenon in a broader political context. James Petras (2007) also points out that there is a direct relation between the growth of NGOs and the decline of living standards; the proliferation of NGOs has not reduced structural unemployment, massive displacements of peasants, nor provided decent wage levels for the growing army of informal workers. Instead, NGOs have provided a thin stratum of professionals with income in hard currency to escape the ravages of the neoliberal economy that affects their country and enabled people to climb up the existing social class structure.

At the time of the writing of this reflection, more than forty years have passed since the emergence of NGOs in Kenya. There is scant literature that is critical of NGOs; this is why Prof. Shivji's efforts are to be applauded.

In 1992, Francis Fukuyama published a book entitled *The End of History and the Last Man*, which became an instant best-seller. In it, he loudly proclaimed the demise of socialism, communism, and Marxism and the definitive triumph of market economics and bourgeois democracy.[1] Market economics seemed to have rejuvenated capitalism as a system. The introduction of Structural Adjustment

---

1 https://www.bolshevik.info/why-we-are-marxists.htm

Programs spearheaded by the IMF and World Bank in Kenya had successfully enabled the state to abdicate its traditional role in economic production and in regulating private economic activity. Kenyan markets opened up to neoliberalism, and the economy let the private sector thrive unregulated, setting clear precedence of economic inequality and crisis as key sectors such as education and health were commodified and privatized. The collapse of the Soviet Union, according to Fukuyama, was proof enough that only one system was possible: the capitalist market economy, and in that sense, history had ended.[2]

Neoliberalism facilitated the integration of African economies into the world capitalist system. But, in less than four decades, defenders of neoliberalism can no longer defend their discourse confidently. Crisis over the last 20 years and particularly the 2008 economic crash and the outbreak of Covid-19 in 2020, have exposed capitalism as a system with no future to talk about.

However, the capitalist system has its own tools and mechanisms to protect itself or deflect its failings to other institutions and shift the blame to another direction to mask its own doing; this is how NGOs come into the picture in assisting in configuring and alienating the root causes of the crisis. For instance, according to Prof. Shivji, "The primary responsibility is placed on the African state for bad governance and lack of accountability, totally ignoring the role of imperialism in the exploitation of African resources." As the state lost the role of providing key services, NGOs stepped in to offer the same services previously offered by the state. As the neoliberal discourse cast the state as the villain, NGOs were able to come in as advisors, consultants, and mentors. While there is no doubt about the impact of corruption and bad leadership by politicians and individuals in government, for the most part, this is just a decoy that serves to shield neoliberalism and capitalism as a system from scrutiny. Corruption and inequality are an inherent part of neoliberalism. It is impossible to talk of economic equality and capitalism in the same sentence!

Prof. Shivji also decries the lack of theorizing within the NGO discourse; there is a tendency in the NGO world to act and not think. Theorization is detested. The result is that most NGOs do not have any grand vision of society, nor are they guided by large issues. Rather, they concentrate on small, day-to-day issues. 'In NGOs, we hardly spend much time defining our vision in relation to the overall social and economic context of our societies. This alienation of issues is where social movements and the NGO discourse differ. Our experiences show that there is a tendency to separate issues within the NGO discourse; water shortage is disconnected from other issues, such as extrajudicial killings and housing, for example. Social

---

[2] https://www.bolshevik.info/why-we-are-marxists.htm

movements and grassroots organizations arm themselves with Political Programs and Manifestos to challenge systematic oppression, while NGOs prefer strategic plans and human rights theory as their blueprint for change.

In our experience, strategic plans that donors proudly fund deflate the agenda of radical social movements. Ideological Social movements leading to popular resistance are usually engaged in a struggle for ideological autonomy from the state, political parties, and the development apparatus. They also have a guiding theory and insist on study sessions to make their cadres ideologically clear. Guiding theories act as a tool to analyze our worldview and history, and theorizing is what enables movements of resistance to not just see history as a mere series of isolated facts but rather as an understood and the interrelated process proved through praxis. Amilcar Cabral writes, 'Every practice produces a theory, and that if it's true that a revolution can fail even though it be based on perfectly conceived theories, nobody has yet made a successful revolution without a revolutionary theory.'

Strategic plans, projects, proposals, and NGO programs have done nothing but depoliticize issues fought for by the masses historically. Under neoliberalism, the human rights discourse displaced national liberation ideologies and social emancipation, turning confrontation into negotiation. Neoliberals have refashioned the idea of freedom by tying it fundamentally to the free market and turning it into a weapon to be used against anticolonial projects worldwide. The push for multi-Party democracy in Kenya involved several agents for change, including progressives and radicals within the resistance movement. Under the 24-year rule of President Daniel Arap Moi, dissidents critiquing his rule were crushed, and most were detained in the infamous Nyayo torture chambers, with others being killed. In the late 1970s and the 80s, at the height of resistance, Marxist- Leninist Movement Mwakenya-DTM emerged and pushed for socialism while castigating Capitalism and its proponents in the government. The left movements paid heavily for challenging President Moi but the emergence of Civil society and NGO human rights organizations carried all the glory for what is now referred to as the "Second Liberation". While progressives were co-opted to work within the human rights framework, they had to tone down their ideology, radical language, and demands such as an end to Capitalism as this would frighten away new-found allies and donors. The method of co-option is still effective today as one way to recruit grassroots activists while depoliticizing their agenda within the neoliberal model. Jessica Whyte in The Morals of the Market: Human Rights and the Rise of Neoliberalism, has pointed out what she sees as some litany of torqued ideological equivalences that today amount to neoliberal moral truisms. For instance:

> Politics are always violent, but the market is always peaceful.
> Freedom is only possible in a market society.
> Human dignity and human inequality are not in contradiction.
> Totalitarianism and redistribution inevitably go hand in hand.
> Imperialism is not the highest stage of capitalism.

The NGO discourse has rehabilitated Imperialism, and the Human Rights theory has been one of its tools to turn radicals into NGO activists. Under the guise of constructive projects, they argue against engaging in ideological movements, thus effectively using foreign funds to recruit local leaders and send them to overseas conferences to give testimonials while effectively encouraging local groups to adapt to the reality of neoliberalism.

NGO activism is misleading as most donor funds come with strings attached. Its own structure is top-down and led by the educated elite who have never experienced any of the issues they proclaim they will solve. Factions are then created within the grassroots movement based on levels of education attained, as those with skills such as writing can write proposals and reports for organizations or get paid for writing articles. It ushers in competition among grassroots activists in a movement that, at its emergence, might have been founded in the spirit of self-reliance, love, equality, and the mission to end oppression. Privilege activism is anti-people and pro-capitalism. Arudhati Roy reiterates, The NGOization of politics threatens to turn resistance into a well-mannered, reasonable, salaried, 9-to-5 job, with a few perks thrown in. Real resistance has real consequences. And no salary

## REFERENCES

Morefield, Jeanne (2020), When Neoliberalism Hijacked Human Rights. Jacobin.

Petras, John (2007), NGOs: In the service of imperialism. Journal of Contemporary Asia. https://doi.org/10.1080/00472339980000221

Pambazuka News. (n.d.). https://www.pambazuka.org/governance/reflections-ngos-tanzania-what-we-are-what-we-are-not-and-what-we-ought-be

Woods, A. (2017, June 22). Why we are Marxists. In Defence of October. https://www.bolshevik.info/why-we-are-marxists.htm

# 8

# Why It's Critical to Study and Understand NGOs

## Irene Asuwa

I applaud Prof Issa G. Shivji's effort in tackling one of the most challenging yet common topics. This a subject we have always tried to address while some of us skirt around it, making many excuses to justify our opportunism and others fairly for their survival., Professor Shivji has attempted to understand the background of our neocolonial states to explain some of the pitfalls that created breeding grounds for this supposedly non-governmental intervention with political and economic interests disguised as non-partisan or non-political. He has also described the big difference between the immediate period after independence and now. One wonders why we are at a worse place and drilling rock bottom despite having all these caring philanthropists and charity organizations trying to make the world a better place for the past decades.

Kenya has had its fair share of deep NGOization, being the backyard of all imperial powers. As Shivji explains in the paper on how these entities follow the same path the colonial powers used to depoliticize and pacify people, numerous NGO boards have a particular clique of people with the power to decide who gets funding and who does not. Moreover, they are the custodians of how modest advocacy should be. So, they indoctrinate those who are 'incapacitated' and have consultants with fat salaries to offer technical assistance (ensure no one veers off from the colonizer's intent) to smaller organizations. Like the state, the NGO sector has its own cartel and elite class, and just like the global imperial clique, they are always trying to edge each other out of the club. There is a silent and, at the same time, the evident class struggle within the sector despite presenting itself as humane. There is significant wage parity between junior colleagues and their superiors. Their labor is overexploited. Some have hostile working conditions and worse zombie workers than the corporates they claim they are different from or are trying to keep in check. There is also massive intellectual labor exploitation and theft under the guise of volunteerism and free internship.

Professor Shivji also points out these private entities' capture of public utilities. They would instead take up what should be state functions than support the people to demand that the state fulfill its obligation. We have many people trained to hold the state accountable. Some of them innocently do it, hoping it would bear fruits, while for others, it is a cash cow to get politicians and consultants into high-end facilities with huge budget lines; for others, it is an outright money-minting scheme. They take the money and report what the donor wants. It has become trendy for duty bearers as they are called to make commitments that they never care to honor. It is a cycle of having one high-end meeting after another, cashing in and signing pledges. Nobody questions them about the embezzlement of these funds the donor community provides; they still fund them anyway. Since the implementors have a condition to work with the government, they 'engage' them to report advocacy 'gains.'

Many people, especially young people, have been blamed for not being part of the policy-making process. Policy-making is a political process; surprisingly, these so-called non-governmental organizations are usually at the very center of it. The government will always say they are waiting on 'development partners' to help them craft, implement and review policies. NGOs have made these processes too expensive and technical for random citizens to afford. We are, therefore, at the mercy of NGOs to access such information and be part of the process passively because most of it, if not all, is often already preempted. The consultants hired by the donors have the document ready, so the passive involvement of a few people is to tick the box. This process alienates the citizen who is a victim of many socioeconomic barriers. There is also the tendency to seek remedies for symptoms without diagnosing the root causes. So, you will be told to pick an issue, but what about the other deeply rotted factors that make it an issue? How sustainable is tackling one problem while turning a blind eye to why it is an issue in the first place? Well, they say we could use the multifaceted approach, but no one wants to comprehensively investigate these problems. Some of these policies are overambitious and impractical under the prevailing political circumstances, which explains why being engaged in the process is for show. They can never be implemented without political goodwill, which can only be a wish in a capitalist state.

Kenya has been at the forefront in propagating elusive neoliberal concepts thanks to the funders of the entities who paint it as a conducive place for foreign investment, the economic powerhouse in the region, and a democratic country with political stability, among other things that come with internalizing concepts such as globalization and the free market. The development partners have created so many white elephant innovation and entrepreneur hubs which are used to blame unemployed and underemployed Kenyans for being choosy and not smart. We have been told to get into business and politics and learn soft skills, but what does it take socioeconomically to do these things? How accessible is capital? How many people can afford to go into politics? How many people can access smartphones, laptops, and reliable internet connections? Before they think of these recommendations, how many have shelter, food, electricity, education, healthcare, and land?

Professor Shivji has not left out the notorious attempts by NGOs to depoliticize very radical ideologies. In this case, Pan Africanism, which was about the unification of the continent, nationalization of natural resources, harmonization of trade, collectivization of agriculture, and having a common currency, among other progressive steps to make Africa better for her people, has been reduced to very liberal and reactionary aims. Some NGOs even claim to be Pan Africanists, and the executive staff ensure they represent that through rhetorical acts like adorning Vitenges in international conferences, throwing in a few African language words, and dropping foreign names but serving capital behind the scenes. These supposed Pan-African NGOs are mostly funded by colonial governments, banks and corporates that continue to plunder the continent. This circus has birthed puppets of imperialism who pose as Pan-Africans while being sponsored by imperial warlords and brokers for natural resources. They put forward a populist nationalistic stance to cover for their actions against the African people.

In this era, social justice and social democracy are the new trendy identities to cover for the openly failed imperialist and capitalistic elusive concepts like democracy, good governance, free market, and the like. It is a comfortable position to take. They do not sound very radical and highly politicized as they would have in the past. As usual, they have been smoothened and made fashionable. Even neo-colonial governments and corporates fund social justice and social democracy work, as they do the opposite. This has offered a very smooth and soft-landing space for imperial powers to infiltrate movements and organizations that might be very vibrant and radical. They have been successfully dehorned and tainted by corporations. At face value, these attempts look very harmless until the smooth operation is done and the organization is muzzled and placed in a dilemma.

Community mobilizers and organizers in this age need to study and understand NGOs for what they are. That way, we shall be able to keep up with the very fast mutations in occurrence and have frank discussions on how to survive within a deeply capitalist environment and still struggle against it because we cannot afford to lose sight of it. Through the culture of study, we can analytically and critically interrogate the danger of being pacified through NGOs and their role. This understanding will also help us creatively explore the question of survival and struggle in a very open manner. How to handle self-sustenance with a sense of our political and economic environment.

# 9

# Against a
# Political Economy of Silence

## Alieu Bah

There are two sites of silence on the African continent that dance into each other in a painful and uneven dialectic. On one side is the muffled, the stuttered and the muted, the one who produces but never gains. On the other side is the one who holds the whip of silence. A powerful, cunning entity but thoroughly deodorized as a holy helper through a laundry stretching centuries. He's proffered as genuinely innocent of the blood that capital comes into the world dripping head to toe with—word to Marx. This dancing arena is a shared space where the thesis and the antithesis, the slave and the master, the toiler and the capitalist, clasp hands and body in a deadly sway that leaves only cascades of misery and grief in its wake.

The work of Issa Shivji *Silences in NGO Discourse* reminds us something of this dance. It contends with the hurtful silence, false neutrality, and sanitized language that feeds the voluntary sector. He argues that. I agree. The fault lines have long been drawn between those who accumulate and those dispossessed. Yet there has been a great battle of hearts and minds to erase this fact in the ongoing lives and afterlives of the African yearning for a new and radiant Africa.

Shivji dissects and dismantles these loud silences and brings a radical language that exposes them. Using a historical materialist analysis, he foregrounds a totality that shatters the issue-based paradigms pushed by those beholden to neoliberalism and its many attendant partisan players in Africa's development processes. Instead, the economic, political and historical are tied together in a brilliant tapestry that shows and proves the necessity of a theoretical understanding of oppression, which the NGO world has refused, is imperative if there is to be any meaningful change in Africa.

The book begins with the history of the plunder that has led Africa to where it is. Why is this important? Why do we have to start by understanding the past? As Shivji said in the book, 'History is about the present. We must understand the present as history to change it for the better; perforce, in the African context, the imperial project is not only historical but the lived present.' Here we are reminded of history as a tool to understand the todays and tomorrows we aspire to, not a mere recollection of the past. Our history here established is to be used in a coherent system of theoretical development to bring about liberation, without which we fight a losing battle as we go a long way and end up wrong.

Then there is the issue of territorial nationalism and Pan-Africanism raised, critical discourse at the forefront of progressive debates regarding the nature and reality of the freedom struggle. Shivji asserts that African nationalism was born in the womb of Pan-Africanism, and truthfully so, as history itself bears righteous witness. An overarching movement whose purpose was and is to span beyond the territory and trauma of the colonial border. A border crafted for extraction, accumulation and surplus value ends up in the imperial core while dialectically impoverishing, dispossessing and stagnating the colonized land.

The colonial boundary is a geographic perversion that leaves the colonized man and woman walking on their heads, rootless and groundless in the lands of their birth and becoming. What, then, is the remedy? What is the starting point of undoing it? A scientific program must ensure that it recognizes the wholeness of both capital and its antithesis, labor. A theory that sweeps the grand totality of the colonial state and its roots in the imperial order. Pan-Africanism becomes the logical conclusion of this effort. Born as it were in the diasporas of Africa, where the descendants of enslaved Africans cannot claim any state created by colonialism as theirs, our ancestors were stolen before it ever was. A fierce ground was and is still held in its development as it vacillates between the idealist and materialist understanding of the social, political and economic. But it is beyond the scope of this review to delve into that exchange.

Shivji reminds us of the dangers of any nationalism not rooted in this Pan-African project. That it will, as it already has given birth to the ugly monsters of chauvinism, xenophobia, and ethnicism, amongst other ills. However, he is clear that this must be a Pan-Africanism of the people that goes beyond the statism that had marred it for a long time. It must be centered on the African people's popular struggles for freedom and liberation. This is an important point as organizers build against the neocolonial state in this neoliberal stage of imperialism — an atomizing ideology that promotes the most insidious individualism even as it fragments intellect and activity.

The silences he speaks of are both chilling and sober in their presentation. But the thesis is clear: NGOs don't occupy a no man's land regarding political stances. They are not bystanders in the neoliberal onslaught of Africa. Shivji posits, and rightly so, that they belong in the heart of the imperial project whose sole mission is profit. Tracing the history of their appearance on the continent to the defeat of the national project, it is clear that it was a calculated effort to stunt both the material gains of the nation-state and the intellectual and ideological direction of the progressive forces. By situating themselves as innocent entities in development issues, they could charge ever-on towards edifying and upholding the ideas of international capital. So today, you find so-called civil society organizations that proclaim non-political, non-partisan postures while busy firefighting symptoms that are all but political and partisan. Amid this organized and intentional confusion, the activist is born. A creature who is never to think or reflect but only to act. He is a friend of the verb —ever doing and working, rarely thinking as he is conditioned to unknowingly uphold the Cartesian dualism of western modernity. Thinking and theorizing are zones he rarely ventures into. Even if he does —the thinking bit— it is never done to guide his struggle but only to fill evaluation forms to keep the imperial masters appraised.

This neoliberal NGO discourse is steeped in building on appearances while it avoids interrogating the undercurrents of what makes a certain phenomenon appears in a given historical conjuncture. An obsession with symptoms that refuses diagnosis of the disease. A classic example today is the climate change movement issued by NGO-backed organizations. For example, there is a massive drive in tree planting across the continent to control the effects of global warming and protect the biosphere. A noble act indeed. However, do these organizations ever question why people cut down those trees in the first place? What is the systemic cause of cutting down trees from the poor side of town or the pillage of entire forests by transnational corporations? Here we are confronted with an underlying problem that flies away from what we see and perceive.

We are forced to contend with a contradiction that we cannot answer without going beyond the moral binary of good and evil. Since if we look too closely, we see the system that impoverishes the poor driving them to cut ancient trees for survival, is the same one that sweeps destructively through entire rainforests. The surplus value that is robbed from the poor becomes the one that causes havoc through cutting a few trees to corporations wiping across tropics of flora and fauna — one trying to survive, the other in constant accumulation. This, if acknowledged, forces one to relinquish the naive notion that painkillers can cure malaria and go about cleaning the breeding area of mosquitoes. Here is a metaphor that sums up something *Silences in NGO Discourse* confronts.

But Shivji is careful not to bunch all actors in this scheme as mere pretenders or selfish benefactors. He recounts those with noble intentions who desire to use these spaces and organizations to change their people's conditions. But he quickly reminds us that good intentions and morals aren't enough to bring about that change if they aren't rooted in understanding the system that creates these monstrosities. This is a point we must ever be cognisant of as neoliberal thought and action now permeate our very consciousness in how we view and envision our struggle. Ours should understand that society is governed by laws rooted in concrete objective reality beyond the mere fickle and fancy of thought and whim. The capitalist mode of production, which gave us the neocolonial state, operates according to its logic. A logic that isn't attendant to any morality but only to profit and power. If these laws aren't studied and understood, then all is left with high-sounding slogans and altruisms that have no power to overturn the squalor we continue to wallow in.

This is a courageous book that invites us to go beyond appearances and phenomena and to seek to understand the underlying realities of anything. It affirms new alternative worlds and a beautiful, free Africa is possible but only when we critically merge theory and practice and take the side of the oppressed and all those pushed out by the powerful. Dare to read this book. Have the courage to think and act on it even as you expand your conclusions in this critical phase of the African Revolution.

# 10

# Organic Intellectuals and the Battle Against Neoliberal Policies in Zimbabwe

## Antonater Tafadzwa Choto

Intellectuals are often considered to be the learned ones; those who have acquired degrees, read books and are aware of world events. In most cases, people relate the word intellectual to those they label 'great thinkers' such as professors, academics, lawyers and scientists. However, writing from prison cells in the early twentieth century, Antonio Gramsci extended the definition of the intellectual to include individuals without qualifications as prescribed by the ruling class. Gramsci undertook the study of intellectuals from a Marxist perspective, analyzing the development of intellectuals in Europe and America. Gramsci further identified that the feudal system developed traditional intellectuals. In the same category, he included those of the capitalist system, thus the economist, scientist and factory technician.

With the success of the Russian October 1917 Bolshevik revolution and the possibilities of socialist revolutions in other European countries, Gramsci concluded that it was significant for the working class to produce its 'organic intellectuals' as a precondition for a socialist transformation of society. In his writings, he constantly interacted the theme of intellectuals with other critical themes such as hegemony, civil society, the war of maneuver and passive revolution. The theme of intellectuals that he further developed in prison continues to resonate with the contemporary working-class struggles. This paper focuses on working-class organic intellectuals in Zimbabwe whose historical role is often overlooked in favor of traditional formal intellectuals.

From the late 1990s to the current period, the Zimbabwean working class has witnessed the rise of Gramscian organic intellectuals who, through their experience in resisting ESAP's neoliberal economic policies and Zanu-PF's authoritarian rule, emerged from the rank-and-file trade union and working-class movements. However, the emerged organic intellectuals have faced challenges brought about by Non-Governmental Organisations (NGOs) that were formed and supported by western governments and their foundations. Massive funding was poured into the Zimbabwean civil society by global neoliberal institutions posing challenges to organic intellectuals who emerged advocating for the overthrow of the capitalist neoliberal policies. NGOs have played a critical role in neutralizing the revolutionary potential of working-class organic intellectuals. The role of the well-funded NGOs, coupled with the continued authoritarian rule by Zanu-PF in the late 1990s, resulted in some of the working-class organic intellectuals becoming what was termed by David Moore (1988) as 'organic intellectuals in transition.' They transitioned into emphasizing democratic and economic reforms as was pushed by the NGOs instead of working towards the total overthrow of the neoliberal ESAPs. This article will look into two incidents relating to the role of NGO funding on organic intellectuals, as it is essential to understand what happened as part of our lessons in working-class resistance.

In 1991, President Robert Mugabe's government abandoned the state welfare policies it had adopted in 1980 during the independence period in favor of the guidelines recommended by the Bretton Woods institutions - the International Monetary Fund (IMF) and the World Bank, thus the Economic Structural Adjustment Programme (ESAP). Mugabe's government defended the neoliberal policies as policies that would stimulate economic growth and raise employment levels based on higher productivity and competitiveness. However, ESAP resulted in reduced economic growth, leading to high unemployment and increased poverty. The failure of ESAP and its adverse effects on the working class led to the 1990s becoming a decade of unprecedented industrial and social action' (Bond and Saunders 2005:45). The students and the township working class, including the unemployed youths and women, joined the resistance initiated by workers. The revolutionary International Socialist Organisation intervened in these struggles, with its ideology further radicalizing the workers. As a result, the emerging working-class organic intellectuals who had started by making economic demands and the overthrow of the neoliberal ESAP evolved into calling for the capture of political power through the formation of a Workers Party. This discontent resulted in middle-class academics, lawyers, and other professionals entering the political battle either as individuals or through the NGOs that employed them or they had founded.

The radical move by the class-conscious organic intellectuals did threaten not only Mugabe's authoritarian government but also local and international capital. Accordingly, the international bourgeoisie responded by intervening in the struggles through NGOs led by the traditional intellectuals, who sought not only to deal with Mugabe's repressive measures but, importantly, to control the radicalization of the organic intellectuals, which threatened the capitalist system in Zimbabwe.

The western Non-Government Organisations (NGOs) such as FES played a role in shifting the focus to the constitutional reform exercise with the hope of removing Mugabe and Zanu PF from power. Hence the National Constitutional Assembly was formed, drawing the debate away from the concrete social structure policy resistance to the Constitutional process. A Working People's Convention was convened by the Zimbabwe Congress of Trade Unions (ZCTU) in conjunction with civic organizations in February 1999 in response to a call for forming a political party. The Convention witnessed conflicting aspirations of organic and traditional intellectuals and ended in the defeat of the organic intellectuals in their call for a Workers Party. A multi-democratic movement was formed, the Movement for Democratic Change (MDC). The focus was now on winning electoral power.

Threatened with the prospect of losing power, Mugabe's Zanu-PF government PF took a leftward shift against imperialist policy and gradually regained the upper hand. Mugabe's government embraced the land invasions by poor Svosve peasants, supported by war veterans. The land re-distribution process was initiated, benefiting the landless peasants and the urban working class who occupied farms in or close to urban areas, turning them into residential stands. The organic intellectuals who had been side-lined or were transiting, by contrast, were unable to initiate serious resistance as the MDC, the movement they supported, took a right-wing shift embracing neoliberal economic policies, which had been the cause of revolts by the working class.

Though the working-class organic intellectuals of the late 1990s into early 2000s in Zimbabwe failed to remove Mugabe's authoritarian government, they managed to show their power against capitalism and neoliberalism. Only the working class, led by their organic intellectuals, successfully challenged Mugabe and the capitalists in the struggles of the late 1990s. Mugabe responded with repression and a partial retreat from the neoliberal policies. In contrast, the capitalists responded by intervening in the struggles and limiting their impact not to threaten their system.

The political and economic crisis in Zimbabwe has continued to worsen due to the economic sanctions imposed on the country and the global crisis of 2008, something that this paper will not go into as it requires in-depth analysis. In November 2017, the masses went out to the streets calling for Mugabe's removal, resulting in his resignation after the army's intervention and his subsequent house arrest. Mnangagwa took over as president the same year. Since then, his government has been making efforts to see the removal of economic sanctions and the receipt of international financial aid, pledging to compensate the white commercial farmers who lost their land during the redistribution process. However, under its finance minister Mthuli, the government continues to implement neoliberal measures under the slogan 'Austerity for Prosperity' and 'Zimbabwe is Open for Business'. The austerity policies have caused massive suffering, and it is common to hear people say that life under Mugabe was better than it is in the new dispensation. On the other hand, the opposition offers no solution to the crisis of neoliberalism.

The working class is now focused on the elections of 2023, where the choice is the possibility of ushering in a new government under the Citizens' Coalition for Change or continued authoritarian rule under Zanu-PF; either way, neoliberal austerity measures will continue. On the one hand, a few local and foreign investors will continue accumulating wealth, especially within the mining sector, where wealth continues to be taken from Zimbabwe. But on the other hand, the western imperialist foundations will continue to pour massive funding into NGOs to derail popular struggles against capitalist neoliberal policies, limiting it to democratic issues, a persistent setback for working-class efforts. This is a contemporary challenge faced by organic intellectuals in Zimbabwe and Africa.

Massive funding by western imperialists to NGOs is used to bribe emerging organic intellectuals and radicals, blunting their struggles against capitalism and limiting them only to democracy and the removal of authoritarian or dictatorial governments. With competition in the job market, the traditional intellectuals who form part of the NGOs' leadership are not concerned and hardly question their funders' ideological intentions or how their discourse contradicts the struggles of the working people against neoliberal policies. Most African local NGOs receive funding from international capitalist forces in Europe and America, the same forces behind the current neoliberal economic policies. It is time for the working-class organic intellectuals of today to move beyond the despair of NGOs operating in the workers' movement and focus on revolutionary theoretical education to movements. The experience of the late 1990s in Zimbabwe and the current role of the working-class organic intellectuals shows that the ordinary working class can make their own history.

# 11

# The Relevance of
# *Silences in the NGO Discourse*
# in Today's Struggle

## Mary Anne Kasina

O ur struggle is rooted historically and must be problematized, historicized and politicized. Therefore, we critically analyze the conception of NGOs as non-governmental, non-political, non-partisan, non-ideological, non-academic, non-theoretical and non-profit. We have to know ideological, economic and political.

Following the defeat of national projects and the rehabilitation of imperial projects, African economies became firmly inserted in the imperialist web or chess board. Moreover, the opportunist imperialists derailed popular struggles by imposing the so-called multiparty democracy and 'good governance', thus reasserting their political and ideological hegemony.

Issa Shivji reiterates that the history of Africa's enslavement must be viewed from the first contact with the Europeans five centuries ago through the slave trade, colonization, and globalization. The development of Europe and America's industrial revolution was facilitated by the exploitation of Africa. The trade in African captives tore apart the social fabric of African society, destroying their internal processes of change.

My reflections on the *Silences in the NGO discourse*, as highlighted by Prof Issa Shivji, in today's context, are as follows.

## THE COLONIAL LEGACY

By slicing the African cake by dividing the African continent into spheres of influence using violence, Africa's natural and human resources were exploited through forced labor, and we have never recovered. This is why we still have severe economic crises and a high unemployment rate. States established by the colonialists cut across 'natural' geographic, cultural, ethnic and economic ties among communities that had evolved historically. What they did was make us have boundaries that were artificially drawn, with rulers literally reflecting the balance of power and strength among imperial states. Boundaries divided up people, natural resources and historical affiliations.

## MENTAL HEALTH AND DEPENDENCY ON NGOS

Mental health among our people has continued to deteriorate due to the dehumanizing effects of the system. The issue of mental health should be viewed as a manifestation of class struggle. In the ongoing COVID-19 era, the economy continues to collapse because we do not own any resources. Production processes rely heavily on coercion rather than on consent, which is characteristic of the capitalist economic system.

We also see NGOs dividing the struggle into clusters and getting data and statistics for more funding from the donor community without giving complete solutions to the problems communities go through in concrete reality. They want numbers; their fight is not change. Until then, shall we continue to document cases in our communities while NGOs are non-political and our issues are political?

## THE BRIDGE TO EMPLOYMENT

This is where we see the issue of doing the same work in the fight against human rights violations in our communities, such as, in the case of the Social Justice Movement, documenting stories of our lived experiences due to our subjection to systemic, structural violence manifested through extra-judicial executions, gender-based violence and femicide while NGOs doing the same work pocket millions of monies resulting from our own reporting.

## THE STRUGGLE OF WOMEN

It is not until women are empowered economically, socially and politically that the system will cease to exploit the labor of women. Giving birth is labor, and due to neoliberalism, life has been privatized, with people failing to afford basic needs. Access to food, water, housing, healthcare and education is difficult. So we have to organize and speak truth to power, as Prof Shivji has done. We must embark on feminism as an ideology towards socialism; for this change to occur, women must be liberated. As Thomas Sankara said, 'there can be no revolution without the liberation of women'.

## COMPLACENCY OF THE MIDDLE CLASS

The state has continued to borrow heavily while human rights violations have increased. This is especially relatable to the exploited people who survive from hand to mouth daily, while the middle class, who are also oppressed by the system, continue to normalize violations because they can meet better material conditions. We all want to live better; our fight is for better material conditions for all.

We want to live as human beings, not in a society that is exploitative and oppressive. This is why we have to question the role of NGOs and understand our role too.

## THE UNITED NATIONS

Hugo Chavez says that the United States should not continue to sit in the UN General Assembly if it does not respect the resolutions made in the assembly. Nevertheless, people have continued to document violations against human rights and tabled the issues at the United Nations, but there is hardly any follow-up or feedback. We thus find ourselves pursuing reforms overlooking the most urgent problems that continue to threaten the existence of humanity.

# 12

# The New Missionaries in Africa

## Rodgers Okakah

When you ask a majority of my countrymen what they understand by the word 'NGO', you will undoubtedly find that the response is close to 'Saviors' of the world; institutions willing to spend donor funding to bring positive change through acts of charity to the less privileged in the society. In my space, defenders of human rights also express this naivety, and a good number also assume that these acts of charity and donations come directly from the coffers of these organizations. Unfortunately, this mindset continues to mislead and confuse even organizers in the struggle, who view these organizations as the best alternative to turn to in the face of poor service delivery by the state.

As we keenly peruse through the pages of history, particularly on the lost decade of the 1980s (as Issa Shivji puts it), we see the expansion of the imperial project in third-world countries and an influx of NGOs as matters of national development take a nose dive into the abyss. 'Tembea nao uwajue', a Swahili adage, loosely translates to 'walk with them to know their ways'; with this I'll therefore give my personal experience working with these new missionaries in Africa and how this debunked my prior amateurish understanding of these new age charity crusaders during this era of neoliberalism.

With keen observation, when we look into the flipside, we realize that the NGO is but a mirror image of the colonial missionary institutions, an appendage of the neoliberal offensive incorporated deep in the heart of underdeveloped countries to compel the masses to consent unconsciously to the bigoted social order. Allow me to illustrate how these institutions actually promote neoliberal policy. NGOs pride themselves as non-governmental, non-ideological, non-theoretical, non-political, but non-nothing, when typically, most of the programs they indulge in are subject to all these forces.

The big NGOs, as I have witnessed, are mostly led by the petty-bourgeois class who enforce policies geared towards implementing the interests of the West. Hence, their loyalty lies away from the poor, working-class people. With imperialist capital trickling in, NGOs grew in stature to become a sector on its own in the economy, a safe haven for retired government bureaucrats and mainstream elites who enjoy this revolving-door neoliberal model of the state, NGOs and corporations.

So how exactly are NGOs abetting the imperial project? As we interrogate deeply, we find that NGOs are a direct antithesis of what they actually stand for. They are institutions registered by the government, performing activities assigned to the government by the electorate, such as dispensing funds and services and using the sponsorship of corporations and foreign governments. Therefore, it beats logic that this same institution is expected to truly quash the social injustices attributed to the neo-colonial system.

In highlighting the contradictions within these organizations, I give a case study of one foundation which borrows its name from a prominent freedom fighter. Established to assist displaced persons during the colonial period to get alternative land and settlement, the institution's administration paints a proper picture of nepotism. The whole management is run by one family, with little or no knowledge of how to actually run an organization. From my observation based on previous encounters with this institution on various events organized by them, the CEO went on to assign herself various roles; a host, master of ceremony, event coordinator, accountant, entertainer and, amusingly, part of the guests of honor, of course with government agencies present. The events ended in chaos.

Through such occurrences, we also get to observe how NGOs work tirelessly to bury the history of our true revolutionaries, diluting their sacrifices for liberation with deeds that defeat everything they stood for.

As a front for imperial powers, NGOs play a critical role in disrupting the organizing of social movements. It is a well-known fact that using foreign capital with a cap of donor limitations has been instrumental in making organizations fighting for social justice dependent on these funds and in further extinguishing them. The moment donor funding starts to flow in, the social structure of the movements changes with it. Where people previously protested in true solidarity for change and patriotism, we see them abandon ship and join protests that only offer a little stipend. When these social movements call for solidarity, members and the community fail to show up if no money exchanges hands.

The NGO programs are also usually single-issue based. Hence they work to solve one symptom of the problems within the society instead of dealing with systemic failure in general. These programs also change periodically, meaning, for example, our struggle today against extrajudicial killings can quickly change tomorrow as advocacy for civic education, or a struggle against gender-based violence, despite not having solved the initial problem. The other observation is that a lot of money is donated to run the programs, but little change is actually felt on the ground. How effective some of these programs are is something we as activists and human rights workers, need to deliberate critically on.

The death of Social Movements can also be attributed to infiltration by government agents through the NGOs. 'The infiltration of social movements is not a new phenomenon,' I remember a comrade narrating to me, 'in 1919, the US government sent agents to destabilize the United Negro Improvement Association, led by Marcus Garvey, and still used the same tactic in the 70s and 80s to surveil and destroy the ranks of the Black Panther Party.' The same tactics are applied today. Typically, social movements exist as informal structures, with the collective from different backgrounds choosing to work organically as the movement grows. When NGOs come into the picture, they distort and disrupt this situation so that we get proposals for hiring consultants from the same NGOs to assist the movement in strategic planning and experts to file reports to get more funding. We sometimes get interns who quickly rise through the movement's ranks and expose its operations.

As I draw to a close, this is a slight detail of the crisis that is the NGOization of Social movements. However, not all is lost in this sea of crisis. I understand that particularly a handful of NGOs might be genuine in their pursuit for real change, and I applaud this cause; nonetheless, their programs would be tantamount to fetching water with a sieve if they don't insist on making them pro-people in their operations. It is important to self-cultivate toward ideological clarity to solve the systemic issue at play.

Down with the Catechists of Aid!

# 13

# The Real Struggle is Class Struggle

## Minoo Kyaa

Non-governmental organizations, or NGOs, are often seen as protectors of human rights that can work towards justice and development to provide a voice for those who may not have one and advocate for change, especially in third-world countries. However, imperialist powers also use NGOs as tools of control rather than protectors of human rights. This way, imperialism uses human rights as an excuse to further its own agenda in underdeveloped states with weak governments, making it difficult to organize toward radical change, especially at the grassroots level. The romanticization of poverty by NGOs has made it extremely difficult for grassroots activists to ideologically organize and educate the community without the small tokens NGOs use to entice poor community members.

I joined the social justice movement back in 2018 and became a member of the Mukuru Community Justice Centre. Having grown up in Mukuru, one of the largest slums in Nairobi, I had witnessed all sorts of oppression by the system, from the lack of water, proper health care and education, to extra-judicial executions, police brutality, misuse of power by state officials, extreme poverty and much more. When I joined the center, I had a few friends with whom I attended NGO forums and activities and received some monies in return. The forums I attended never advocated for radical change; most of them were dialogues with local authorities about issues that affected the community. These dialogues did not change anything, really; situations remained the same, and communities continued to suffer. I now see the imperialist ploy; use NGOs to collect data in poor communities for their own records and make sure the community maintains hope rather than fighting for itself to bring permanent radical change, which is socialism.

Gacheke Gachihi, a member of Mathare Social Justice Centre, was one of the people who convinced me to join the movement after he narrated his horrifying experiences with the police at a tender age while working in a car wash in Kiamaiko, Nairobi, and how he managed to speak out against the injustices. This eye-opening session helped me understand how our struggles are interconnected. The idea of many communities forming a united front to fight against injustice looked more workable to me than what NGOs offered. Most of the young people who had accompanied me on that day did not see the bigger picture, including the one who had invited me to the session; rather they complained because we did not receive money as usual but just one packet of maize flour. They swore to never again attend a social justice activity.

Imperialism uses mental slavery to thrive. Clearly, NGOs are a tool of imperialism to continuously maintain docility among the proletariat; to make the class lose hope and therefore rigid and impossible for them to think beyond the small tokens given to them. I could not stop thinking about how our struggles are interconnected, so I immediately joined Mukuru Community Justice Centre. I was invited to an activity where I learned about a community in the Philippines that kicked out all the NGOs in their area when they discovered the limitations of NGO work and the human rights theory, which was being used as a weapon to romanticize poverty and exploit their labor. Coming from a community that is overwhelmed by 'reformism', the struggle became more relatable.

NGOs have completely distanced themselves from the real struggle, which is the class struggle. They have ignored the issue of mental slavery, which is the most powerful weapon that neo-colonialism is using to maintain its power. NGOs have many limitations, making it difficult to organize a conscious mass of people. They never talk about political ideology, our greatest tool for revolution, and they have refused to unify our struggle. They have divided the struggle into too many portions, such as having one NGO dealing with extrajudicial killings, another dealing with menstrual poverty, another one for mental health and others for women's empowerment while all this falls under capitalism. Our struggle is primarily the class struggle, which is the principal contradiction.

NGOs are a way for the oppressor to maintain their power by keeping the oppressed in check. They offer little more than a Band-Aid solution to systemic problems; change can only happen through mass mobilization and organized struggle. It is important for us as revolutionaries to be critical of NGOs and their discourse and to remember that the real struggle lies in the fight against capitalism. Only then shall we achieve liberation. The proletariat must unite under a guided communist ideology to fight for permanent change. Our struggle lies in the fight against capitalism. Only then shall we achieve liberation.

# 14

# Day and Age of
# Donor-Driven Policies

## Gerald Kamau

In this current era of neoliberalism, we are seeing a flourishing of non-governmental organizations (NGOs), like the new missionaries to Africa. Some NGOs come with programs imposed in Africa by international financial institutions and 'development' agencies.

Between 1984 and 1994, the United Kingdom increased its funding to NGOs by almost 400 percent, to £68,700,000. Countries like Australia, Finland, Norway and Sweden also increased official NGO funding, leading to a mushrooming and growth of NGOs. The continued growth of NGOs saw them become an integral part of the system that sacrifices respect for justice and rights, taking the 'missionary' position to soften the masses while the State violates them.

When I first interacted with NGOs, I lost my conscious revolutionary spirit. Since my first Saba Saba March for our Lives demonstration in July 2019, I have been dreaming of change. However, NGOs have infiltrated our activist spaces. Comrades have lost the zeal to fight. They feel exploited, wasted and alienated from the community they come from.

Prof. Issa Shivji has analyzed the pitfalls within the NGO discourse and the destructive effects of neoliberal policies in Africa, neocolonial Africa under the comprador class who, after more than 50 years, continue to oppress the masses through violent ways of the oppressor. He also examines the self-style descriptions of non-governmental, non-profit, non-political, non-partisan, non-ideological, non-academic, non-theoretical, or so non-nothing.

The NGOs here stand for nothing. Thus, we question their mandate and role in the structures of class struggles if they are not the 'modern-day missionaries'. Africa is another form of slavery perpetrated by the imperialists through the help of NGOs, where national projects fail, and imperial projects are rehabilitated. Shivji points out the prominence and privileging of the NGO sector in the womb of the neoliberal offensive. Its aims are ideological, economic, and political.

European nations began exploiting Africa through slavery and colonization from the fifteenth century to the late nineteenth century. This paved way for the European powers to build up their economies with resources stolen from Africa through genocide, domination, exploitation, and humiliation. They demarcated boundaries in Africa, dividing people through tribal lines, cultural outlooks, languages, and systems of education that were alien to native Africa. This resulted in export-oriented economies based on the export of raw materials and the import of manufactured goods. By dividing people along ethnic, religious and racial lines, the oppressor cemented his invasion tactics. The missionaries were also used by the colonial state to preach Christianity so that Africans could be softened to submit to their rule. The indigenous religion of our forefathers was condemned as primitive. Religion and education also became vehicles for reproducing colonial racial and cultural complexes; white as superior and black as inferior. The white man's beliefs were 'religion', the black man's were 'witchcraft' or 'black magic'; the white man's communication was language, and the black man's was dialect.

The history of Africa was the ideological genesis of African Nationalism which was central in Pan Africanism. However, Nationalism in post-colonial Africa degenerated into statism, politically authoritarian and economically rapacious. Under neocolonialism, the state became an instrument of private accumulation. The neoliberal offensive in Africa used institutions like the 'donor community' and multinationals to serve its own interest while turning a blind eye to mismanagement and corruption.

During the 1970s, the neo-colonial states of Africa borrowed heavily, whether for genuinely productive or for prestige projects. Cheap loans became unbearable, plunging African countries into deep crises. Social services declined as infrastructure deteriorated, with African governments pleading at the IMF's doors and the Paris Club. The 1980s marked the beginning of developmentalism's decline and neoliberalism's rise (globalization). Colonialism had left through the front door and returned through the back door in the form of neo-colonialism. Visionary leaders, such as Kwame Nkrumah, Ben Bella, Patrice Lumumba, Pio Gama Pinto, and Thomas Sankara, were assassinated or overthrown. At the same time, the likes of Jomo Kenyatta, Daniel Arap Moi, Houphet Boigny, and Leopold Senghor became accomplices of imperialism.

Policymaking, an important aspect of sovereignty, has been wrenched out of the hands of African states and placed in the hands of the so-called stakeholders, such as NGOs. It is pegged on private capital, which translates into foreign private capital as the 'engine of growth' in Africa. It banishes issues of equality and equity to the realm of rights rather than development.

The notion of portraying African countries as poor and hence represented by the NGOs is highlighted by Shivji. The paper explains that the sudden rise of NGOs and their apparent prominent role in Africa is part of this neoliberal, organizational and ideological offensive. In 1980, civil society came into vogue, with the term civil society organization used interchangeably with NGO. NGOs are presented as the 'third sector', the other two sectors being the State - power and politics, and the Private sector - capital and economics.

The concept of civil society in European history represented a transition from a medieval feudalist to a capitalist society, part of the bourgeois-democratic revolution. The so-called civil society, in the sense of the public sphere of production, is not a harmonious whole; but a terrain of contradictory relations between classes, the two poles being the producer class and the proprietor class. Whoever controls production also controls political power, which is the State.

The five minutes of silence in the NGO discourse, as highlighted by Prof Shivji in the African context, are as follows.

1. NGOs in Africa were born in the womb of the neoliberal offensive, which saw greater exploitation and inequality. The anti-state stance of the so-called donor community was the real cause of the upsurge in NGO activities.

2. NGOs are comprised of the educated elite. They are located in urban uptown areas. Prof Shivji outlines the composition of the NGO elite as;
   - Radical elite - previously involved in political struggles with an explicit vision for change and transformation. Politically motivated, they saw the NGO's space as a perfect haven to thrive.
   - Morally motivated - the well-intentioned individuals driven by altruistic motives to improve the conditions of their fellow human beings and compatriots.
   - Mainstream elite - former government bureaucrats who shifted to the NGO's world once they found that donor funding was being directed there. Their motivation is careerist driven by material conditions.

3. NGOs are donor-funded. They do not have any independent source of funding. Thus their work is exercised in relation to donor agendas which vary from NGO to NGO depending on the perspective of its leadership.

4. Advocacy NGO - They focus on particular areas such as human rights, gender, development, environment, and governance. They may respond to the needs of the people but most of them are donor-driven and advance the interests of the donor community.

5. Most NGOs may insert in their charters a vision or mission statement; these are often vague, amorphous and meaningless, such as 'poverty reduction'.

The NGO Discourse of today triumphs on and emphasizes privileged activism. The requirements of funding agencies subtly discourage, if not exhibit outright hostility to, a historical, social and theoretical understanding of development, poverty and discrimination - Act, don't think, and we shall fund you. NGO activism is presented and based on an 'act now, think later' mantra.

My conclusion is that the roles and actions of NGOs promote neoliberalism in the interest of global imperialism and that NGOs are accomplices to exploitation and neo-colonialism.

# 15

# Self-criticism, Contemplation, and Soul-searching

## Ezra Otieno

Non-governmental organizations are pervasive in most people's life. It should thus be basic logic to analyze NGO operations to determine their precise political purpose in the neoliberal international system, but this is not always the case. In response to this cognitive vacuum, Issa Shivji, a law professor at the University of Dar es Salaam, explains in his excellent pamphlet, *Silences in NGO Discourse: The Role and Future of NGOs in Africa*, the urgent need for such critical inquiries. NGOs are now an essential component of a system that compromises regard for justice and human rights. I give the following ideas on NGOs in the spirit of self-criticism, contemplation, and soul-searching as was viewed by Shivji.

Professor Shivji states:

> Before I begin, I must make two confessions. First, my paper is undoubtedly critical, sometimes ruthlessly so, but not cynical. Second, this criticism is also self-criticism, since the author has been involved in NGO activism for over 15 years. Finally, I must make clear that I do not doubt the noble motivations and good intentions of NGO leaders and activists. But we do not judge the outcome of a process by the intentions of its authors. We aim to analyze the objective effects of actions, regardless of their intentions.

Shivji accurately diagnoses that the expansion of the non-profit sector is strongly linked to neoliberal growth imperatives, which have relegated concerns of equality and equity to the realm of rights rather than development. As a result, 'rights' are limited to the domain of lobbying NGOs rather than becoming a field for public resistance.

While such problematic rhetoric has been aggressively contested academically and in the public, Shivji observes that 'a substantial portion of the African intellectual elite has been co-opted and accommodated inside the neoliberal language.' As a result, he argues that 'the rapid emergence of NGOs and its seeming important position in Africa is part of this neoliberal onslaught'. He states that non-governmental organizations (NGOs) reflect the continued rule of imperialism in a new form.

We can see how NGOs are heavily involved in the neoliberal assault on democracies; the 'anti-state position of the so-called donor community has been the main driving force behind the increase in NGO activity. 'They are top-down organizations headed by the bourgeois or their sympathizers. They are headed and primarily constituted by the educated elite', which Shivji has divided into three groups: those who have 'previously engaged in political struggles', altruistic persons who are 'morally driven,' and a popular 'careerist' elite driven by personal aspirations.

As the impact of NGOs has grown, their position has come under more criticism. While NGOs have gained favor with the donor agencies, this growing favor has created a distrust of NGOs among many proponents of dramatic change in the direction of greater equality and socialism. In light of their growing clout, we must ask ourselves whether non-governmental organizations (NGOs) can significantly contribute to change efforts, as we can learn from the book.

Their beliefs and reasons have been summarized in three components, which I have referred to as popular livelihoods, popular participation, and popular power. By 'popular', Shivji means the society's exploited and downtrodden classes and groupings. This is in contrast to the present degrading and utterly ineffective neoliberal rhetoric, in which popular classes are branded the 'poor', to be endlessly investigated and targeted with poverty-relief monies. The term 'popular' refers to the working class's major role in the battle to reclaim the country. To summarize, I think these aspects represent the ideals and issues with which NGOs and activists would connect, as Shivji puts it. However, I believe that many NGOs have failed to consistently advocate for these principles, putting themselves in jeopardy.

To better comprehend NGOs, in our case Kenya, we must first define what they are, what they are not, and what their limits are. For starters, most of their non-governmental organizations (NGOs) are top-down organizations run by elites. Furthermore, the majority of them are concentrated in cities. NGOs did not begin as a reaction to most working people's perceived needs. True, many of us in the NGO world have good intentions and would like to contribute to some cause, whatever we define it. It is also true that many non-governmental organizations (NGOs) address some of the legitimate issues of working people. However, we must acknowledge that we did not grow as, and have yet to become, organic to most people.

Shivji continued to show how elitist NGOs are in that they are not constituencies or membership organizations. Even if they have a membership, it is mostly composed of other powerful people. As a result, their accountability is restricted and limited to a small number.

They end up being more accountable to their funders than to their members, much alone to their constituents.

We have been raised in the 'NGO world' to think that we should act rather than theorize. Theorizing is despised. As a result, most NGOs do not have a big vision of society, nor are they led by huge concerns; instead, they focus on little, day-to-day difficulties. We seldom spend time in NGOs clarifying our vision about our nations' wider social and economic environment. Most of us confuse non-governmental organizations (NGOs) with civil society organizations, weakening conventional member and class-based working-class organizations such as trade unions, peasant groups, etc. We may give a voice to people's organizations (POs). Still, in practice, they and our donors favor NGOs, which has far-reaching repercussions, including weakening representative mass organizations.

The major strength of non-governmental organizations (NGOs) is considered their continuous, principled, and dedicated position in favor of the masses as well as human ideals and issues. We, as revolutionaries, are not a slew of self-serving bourgeois bureaucrats who, by contrast, are motivated by power rather than ideals. We are not even in the business of brokering power, where expediency and compromise reign supreme. We have a mission to oppose and expose the ugliness of power. We are guided by profoundly held human values and causes, and our work is shaped by them.

Non-governmental organizations (NGOs) may serve an important purpose in pursuing reform. But first, we must acknowledge what they are not. I argue that, in our country's current environment of neoliberalism, NGOs have indeed been cast in a surrogate position that most of us have learned to embrace and maybe even felt flattered by. That's where our limits collide, and there is a risk that we shall both take a position that does not belong to us while failing to perform the one for which we are most prepared.

I propose that NGOs and organizers take a close look at themselves. They must take stock of their actions. They must assess themselves in light of their beliefs, ideals, and goals to improve the world. If another universe is feasible, which it is, we must first understand our current one. Not only should we understand the current reality, but we must also understand who keeps it running. Why and how does this world continue to reproduce itself, for whose interest, and for what reason? We must pick sides; those of us who are fighting for a better world versus those who want to keep the current one.

In conclusion, I recommend this book to all leftist organizers. It is a must-read for them. In a neo-colonial state like ours and with the constant aggression of imperialism, comrades need to ground themselves so they are not co-opted by NGOs.

# 16

# Community Organizing and NGOs

## Mary Njeri

During President Daniel Arap Moi's era, there were very few Non-Governmental Organizations (NGOs) in Kenya. They were also not that vibrant due to the measures put then by the dictatorship to muzzle any criticism of the regime. However, things would change in 2002 when President Mwai Kibaki rose to power, having won the elections with strong support from civil society organizations. NGOs then continued to expand in the country, some of which had a focus on advocacy, governance, and human rights as the political atmosphere became more conducive for their operations. Since then, there has been a rapid growth of NGOs in the country, and they have impacted the country both positively and negatively, particularly as regards the struggle for human rights and social justice, where they interact with social movements in community organizing.

NGOs receive funding from donors for different programs within their course. Programs to address different issues such as the water crisis, health, corruption, and extra-judicial killings. There have been positive outcomes following years of campaigns for reforms in particular sectors, such as the push for a reduction in police brutality and the campaign to enable the people to understand their power within the constitution. Nevertheless, there is never an end to these issues, particularly in informal settlements, as the issues are systemically rooted in the global capitalist oppressive system. The NGO discourse does not give such a broad outlook on these issues. In their work, they interact with community organizers who act as their partners on the ground within the communities. Most community organizers and activists are tasked with collecting data on issues such as extra-judicial killings and governance. Also, community organizers play the role of mobilizers for events and forums. The constant cycle within the NGO discourse reduces community organizers to data collectors and mobilizers in the long run, thus alienating them from the masses. The collection of data is used as evidence of NGO work to receive more funding from donors. The funds hardly trickle down to communities, as most of it is consumed within organizations, with their staff taking home heavy packages in salaries and allowances. They are also mostly headquartered in middle-class environs which sometimes can be intimidating for those coming from the slums to access. Further, by using money to organize community forums, the NGOs have created a dependency syndrome that greatly affects the work of community organizers and social movements that don't give any resources for such forums.

NGOs usually present themselves as saviors within communities as regards the solving of societal issues and the provision of public utilities. With this, they often gain the trust of the community. However, instead of tackling issues affecting the whole society, they choose a specific issue, then fundraise as much as possible for it and only change course when funding declines. They can, for example, focus on documentation for extra-judicial executions but shy away from addressing the root cause of the problem: unemployment among the youth. The presentation of Human Rights theory as a soft statement that only requires conventions and reforms for their realization creates the idea that for things to change, we only need to be loyal to systems of oppression and negotiate for change within instead of expanding human rights as a radical discourse which involves not only conventions and reforms but also resistance.

Prof Shivji's paper is important as it sparks an often-overlooked conversation in Kenya and the Global South. The Organic Intellectuals Network, in its efforts to advance this conversation, organized a seminar in Mathare, Nairobi, to discuss this paper with the community at the grassroots level. During the seminar, several critical points were raised:

• NGOs create donor dependency and make it difficult to revolt effectively. USAID is disingenuous in community organizing because it is funded by the USA, a capitalist entity.

• NGOs make us less critical of imperialism.

• NGOs help in driving reforms but they play no part in revolutionary work. We are enslaved to the community projects initiated by NGOs.

• NGOs limit and discourage direct confrontation with governments, reducing the militancy of activists and changing their focus.

• NGOs create bureaucracy with their structures and demands.

• NGOs do not address the root causes of oppression, yet they claim to be providing the solutions. For example, what is the root cause of water scarcity, malnutrition, and extra-judicial executions? An organization might focus on documentation for these issues but fail to consider practical ways to ensure they are avoided.

• NGOs take advantage of the poverty in the slums.

• The government's failure to work for its citizens legitimizes the need for NGOs. For example, in Kibwezi, after multinationals

destroyed the soil and created a dependency on GMO products, NGOs took the stage to fundraise for the farmers.
• NGOs exploit the labor of their employees by putting them under contract with meager compensation.
• NGOs focus on single-issue struggles and alienate skilled individuals from the community, making it difficult to consolidate our gains. Additionally, they may criminalize movements and profile them negatively for them not to be funded whenever differences arise.
• NGOs get their power from our imagined lack of agency fed to us by the capitalist education system.

We need to reject the notion that the solution lies outside of ourselves.

# 17

# Limitations of the NGO Discourse

## Sam Gathanga

The discourse of NGOs has been unclear since their rise in the early 1980s. Like the colonial missionaries who came with the bible in one hand and a gun in the other, the NGOs came with altruist gospel while bidding for their governments. Prof Shivji's *Silences in the NGO Discourse* is a self-critique from an insider perspective.

The book explains why the rise of NGOs during the final stages of colonialism wasn't coincidental but a purposeful plan by the colonial powers to have a back door through which they could return. As Africans were busy celebrating the new dawn for independent countries and the exit of their former colonial masters, NGOs were being established deep within the belly of neo-colonialists and imperialists. The logic brought forth was that young African states needed 'development partners' to help them in their new journey. The master's point was that Africa could not develop by itself, so she needed development partners for their much-needed 'expert opinion'. Africa could not solve her problems on her own; she needed a helping hand. This notion has continued to be perpetuated by the former colonial powers, pointing at the rampant corruption cases, massive unemployment, malnourished populations and other setbacks as justifications for the same, tactically ignoring the fact that these problems exist precisely because of neo-colonialism.

The book starts by explaining the catch-22 situation faced by our founding fathers at the dawn of independence of our African states. They saw the need for a united Africa, and some, like Julius Nyerere of Tanzania, were ready to delay the independence of their countries to allow the formation of an East African Federation, which would then be used to push for the unification of the whole continent. They saw the danger that was to befall the weak and independent nation-states. History proved them right, as the infamous divide and rule are still being used to date in setting one nation-state against the other.

From the imperialist belly, the 'Third Sector' was born. It came with a non-governmental, non-political, non-ideological and non-profit veneer and, with a few deeds of altruism through 'giving back to the community', they were welcomed with open arms just like the early missionaries. They came with the promise to fight poverty and inequality, provide social services to the marginalized poor and bring them back into the mainstream economy. With a rosy picture painted on the wall that could be seen by everyone, a utopian life promised, our governments fell for the trap set by our colonial masters through the third sector. With a lot of funding from their governments, their work in the Global South increased, enabling them to set a strong foothold in the communities. This firmly established the NGO as the third sector complementing the two other sectors; State (political power) and the private sector (capital and the financial engine). The biggest irony in the NGO discourse in the developing world is that their intentions are very political and ideological, and they work for the interests of the big corporations and the governments that sanctioned them.

Prof Shivji explains why all the 'nons' in the civil and NGO verbiage are but a false veneer that peels off quickly when the interests of their donor organizations and governments are not met or are put at stake. He points out the blind spots in the NGO discourse that make their intent and mission unclear. Being the foot soldiers of imperialist power, NGOs have completely engaged in political processes such as policy making as experts offering the 'expert opinion' or acting as development partners.

*Silences in the NGO Discourse* unmasks the altruistic intent painted by most NGOs. It shows how their funding is channeled into compartmentalized programs that are fixed on strategy papers rather than on helping the communities get to the root of their problems by approaching their problems holistically. These programs are donor controlled and involve the communities in a superficial way in trying to undo the injustices they face. The beneficiaries are not allowed to question why their natural resources, such as minerals, do not benefit them. They need to be allowed to find out why some essential services are commodified. Their part is accepting the inflexible projects and programs tailor-made for them by their true friends. At the end of the strategic plan, the masses are left with very little to smile about as they go back to their way of life with nothing solved. At the end of it is a poor community alienated from its true history and what remains is a continuous cycle of poverty that can't be broken since no one is willing to dig into the past and uproot the whole tree and its roots.

Prof Shivji highlights these NGOs' significant role in destroying leftist movements in Africa and Latin America. By presenting themselves as development partners, they win the confidence of these groups, and within no time, the hitherto radical groups change their cause to donor-driven projects. At the end of the project are fragmented and divided groups with a lost cause.

Shivji ends his paper with an introspection of the NGO spaces. It is an insider critique to check and take stock of our work in our communities lest we be the foot soldiers for our imperial masters in London, Paris, Glasgow, Stockholm, Washington or Berlin.

Importantly, this dissertation and the reflections are not a vote of doubt to those in the NGO space. It is a self-introspection analysis of the role we should be playing in bringing a transformational agenda to the oppressed rather than parading them for study and experimentation programs.

# Afterword

## Jörg Wiegratz

NGOs often say they are pro-people and want society to change for the better –a society with far less poverty, inequality, injustice, indignity, and exclusion. There are many NGOs in Kenya, and some of them are present when important matters are discussed. NGOs can be well-funded and vocal and come with plenty of analyses, data, recommendations and plans. Some of them have a fleet of cars, nice offices, Twitter accounts, and good networks. Not all, of course. NGOs speak, and they are listened to. They regularly interact with people in power –the government; and they have partners at home and abroad: funders, well-wishers, and supporters. And yet: a significant proportion of what NGOs say they want  to address and fight against does not really seem to change: poverty remains high and so does inequality, corruption, workers' exploitation, insecurity and humiliation. The change for the better seems not to materialize. There is in some aspects, hardly any change, or even a worsening of the situation for the people. And yet NGOs keep inviting people to workshops, making calls to people to participate, to report, to demand change, to hold others accountable, to express their voice, to work for and believe in change.

So what is going on with these NGOs? What are they doing or not doing? How to make sense of them and their ideologies, funding, influences, programs and meetings, managers and staff? Are they allies or enemies of the wretched of the earth? Should they be engaged with and trusted by the left? Or should they be ignored and kept at a distance, to be scrutinized and fought and campaigned against? Are their diagnoses and prescriptions concerning society's problems wrong? Are NGOs ill-intentioned? Are they not to be blamed for the negative effects of their work? Are they altruistic, badly informed and managed? Are they unlucky, naive, sell-outs or Trojan horses? Are they just data collectors for foreign donors and the Kenyan state? Is the ongoing crisis in society also their fault? Are they pro-system or against it? Are they a force of unity, strength and victory for the wretched, or a force that divides, weakens and lures them in wrong directions, a force that clarifies or fools, speeds up or slows down the struggle for real change, the journey towards liberation and emancipation from oppression and exploitation? And: Do they enable or tame radical social movements and people's struggles? Tricky questions?

JÖRG WIEGRATZ

To confront, think through and debate these questions is vital for left activists, analysts and intellectuals. These questions —and the larger issues they raise —are perplexing and difficult to think through. The accounts in this wonderful book about NGOs in Kenya tell us tells us that it requires a strong sense of history and politics, reality and theory, of self-reflection and self-criticism, individually and collectively. To reflect on the roles, work, dynamics and limitations of NGOs in Kenya, that is, in capitalist Kenya, is far from straightforward because NGOs in a capitalist society are such tricky entities to analyze, much like education or culture. Understanding NGOs, for the left, is also similar in terms of trickiness and importance to understanding media, elections, and courts in capitalism. For example: does the education system stabilize or -challenge existing social relations? \. NGOs are the core institutions of today's capitalist civilization. Understanding NGOs properly helps; misreading them, analytically and politically, has a cost.

And the analysis of NGOs is far from straightforward because such an analysis is personal. The authors in this book know many NGOs, have partnered with, worked for and perhaps liked some of them at some point. Analyzing NGOs is, thus perhaps - in some way - something like analyzing one's family or doing straight talk with someone one has mixed feelings about a complex, difficult relationship. Some NGOs are family. Some people whose ideals, perspectives and on-the-ground work are respected in the left work in the NGO sector and have made a significant, positive difference in people's lives and have given hope to many. They are leaders, mentors, and elders. So, again, it is tricky. Sincere intellectual and personal reflection, and an open conversation, are all required to collectively get a better grip on the matter. This book offers that in plenty.

In sum, comprehending NGOs in capitalism in the 2020s from a left perspective is a tricky-yet-vital intellectual task and a political activity that we cannot do without. Doing so advances ideological clarity - the authors make that very clear. Remaining alone with one's questions and doubts or letting the NGO-isation process run 'unchecked', remaining uncritically involved in its perpetuation, are not really options. Collectively grappling with this, making sense of NGOs in the context of neoliberalism, neocolonialism and imperialism is political; exploring the relationship between NGOs and imperialism is political. To nurture an analytical, critical stance toward the role and impact of NGOs in the capitalist social order is political. And putting all that analysis of NGOs on paper and publishing it is political too, and rare these days and thus to be loudly applauded.

Against this background, this book is a much-needed, unique and useful collective intervention, conversation and reflection of left activists and intellectuals from Nairobi who are connected as comrades via their work with various Social Justice Centers and other radical-left organizations in the city. They write in this book about the realities of the NGO sector in capitalist Kenya and their experiences, views and feelings about them. They do this via engagement with a key left critique of NGOs, Silences in the NGO Discourse: The Role and Future of NGOs in Africa, by Professor Emeritus Issa Shivji (University of Dar Es Salaam, Tanzania). As Maryanne Kasina writes: 'We critically analyze the conception of NGOs as non-governmental, non-political, non-partisan, non-ideological, non-academic, non-theoretical and non-profit'.

In the activists' texts, we find critical reflections about NGO buzzwords and ideologies, about the relationships between NGOs and grassroots movements, including the various consequences for movements of working with NGOs and donors. We find critical reflections about issue-based activism and shallow NGO analysis that often offers remedies for problems without proper diagnosis of causes. That is, for example, without reference to the relationship between the 'issues' NGOs focus on (poverty, state violence, mental suffering, gender inequality etc.) and the twin forces of capitalism and imperialism.

We learn about issues such as careerism in the NGO sector, opportunism, co-option, competition for payments (for work, participation etc.), and the struggle for an economic livelihood as an activist. We also read about the elite class and cartels of the NGOs sector, about the elite's detachment from the realities of the wretched, and about the class struggle, inequality, hierarchies, exploitation and cashing-in practices inside the respective organizations. There is an analytical focus on the influence on radical organizations and movements, on the role of the state and its agents, of political parties and election campaigns, and agents of imperial powers that infiltrate respective groups. As Nicholas Mwangi notes, they use human rights discourse to 'turn radicals into NGO activists ... and encourage local groups to adapt to the reality of neoliberalism'. NGOs have undermined agendas of radical liberation, the national project and the class struggles of the oppressed, and helped rehabilitate imperialism in Kenya, Mwangi, Kasina and Minoo Kyaa observe. 'NGOs have a lot of limitations hence making it difficult to organize a conscious mass of people. They never talk about political ideology, which is our greatest tool for revolution, and they have refused to unify our struggle', Kyaa writes, for example.

In line with Shivji's analysis, the authors in this book highlight the negative stance and ridicule donors and sections of NGOs and movements regarding theory in general and critical, bigger-picture analysis in particular, concerning the systemic, structural issues related to the operations of capitalism and imperialism, or the interconnectedness of social struggles. They also cover the closely related aspects of the NGO functions, politics and power in the neoliberal system: the weakening, diluting, divisionary (e.g. faction-creating) effects NGOs can often have on grassroots movements and organizations and their ideologies and struggles. They discuss the mainstreaming, pacification, depoliticization and demobilization of movements, that is, reducing radical-progressive causes and visions to neoliberalism-compatible aims and objectives. They discuss the attempts to pressure people's struggles into NGOs' ideologies, discourses, annual plans, log frames, dialogue-with-the-authorities-workshops, and liberal reformism. What many authors in the book agree on is the very particular political effect of the neoliberal age of NGOs, civil society and 'good governance' on left-radicalism; they note a de-radicalization, a toning down in analysis and political demands, a continuation of anti-radicalness of Kenyan politics in the 1970s and 1980s, as noted by Mwangi. NGOs, Ezra Otieno argues, also contribute to the 'weakening of representative mass organizations in the country.

The respective analyses provide useful terms, such as 'movement-building industrial complex' or 'donor trap', and analytical insights and statements, such as: 'privilege activism is anti-people and pro-capitalism (Mwangi), or 'NGOs have completely distanced themselves from the real struggle, which is the class struggle. They have ignored the issue of mental slavery, which is the most powerful weapon neo-colonialism is using to maintain its power' (Gerald Kamau), and 'NGOs are a tool of imperialism to continuously maintain docility among the proletariat' (Kyaa). Or: Mwangi's characterization of neoliberal discourses that 'cast the state as the villain' (in the context of corruption and bad leadership), as, for the most part, 'just a decoy that serves to shield neoliberalism and capitalism as a system from scrutiny'.

The existing NGOs-movements relationship has problematic implications for people's struggles in general and the far-left in particular, writes Sungu Oyoo and :

Over time, these movements, just like the NGOs they are replicating, have worked on several issues without sufficiently tackling any single issue – and 'communities are again left grappling'. In this theatre, 'issue-oriented' movements are encouraged. In contrast, cohesive mass movements capable of analyzing the issues and their underlying basis are referred to as radical and locked out of spaces....Many young people who genuinely wish to see a better world and who join these movements – whether they regard themselves as activists, organizers or community leaders – are tunneled into a framework of organizing that discourages theory, either explicitly or implicitly.

Oyoo diagnoses a deep crisis in certain movements:

Within such movements, cadres engaging in critical analysis are often-time ridiculed or dismissed as 'show-offs', or 'wasomi'. In this quagmire, backward elements within the movements push them toward the all-too-familiar path of donor theory and log frames. Words like revolution, freedom, class struggle and Pan-Africanism are every once in a while thrown into this pot of confusion. Such movements are the embodiment of organized chaos, the dance to nowhere that today characterizes the African revolution.' And further 'Movement work and movement-building... have become a full-blown economic activity camouflaged in slogans. Anything and anyone that stands in the way of these slogans is pushed aside, ridiculed, humiliated, intimidated, suspended, or expelled from the movement.' And he asks 'But why this?

This and other productive questions are discussed fruitfully via dialogue with Shivji's analysis. Shivji's account from the 2000s – regarding funders of NGOs' discouragement, if not, in Shivji's words, 'outright hostility to a historical, social and theoretical understanding of development, poverty and discrimination', is confirmed many years later, in the 2020s in Nairobi. Otieno, for example, notes: 'We have been raised in the 'NGO world' to think that we should act rather than theorize. Theorizing is despised. As a result, most NGOs do not have a big vision of society, nor are they led by huge concerns; instead, they focus on little, day-to-day difficulties. We seldom spend time in NGOs clarifying our vision about our nations' wider social and economic environment.' Relatedly, Mwangi analyses:

> Social movements and grassroots organizations arm themselves with Political Programs and Manifestos to challenge systematic oppression while NGOs prefer strategic plans and human rights theory as their blueprint for change. In our experience, strategic plans that donors proudly fund deflate the agenda of radical social movement...Strategic Plans, Projects, Proposals, and NGO programs have done nothing but depoliticize issues fought for by the masses historically. Under neoliberalism, the human rights discourse displaced ideologies of national liberation and social emancipation, turning confrontation into negotiation....While progressives were co-opted to work within the human rights framework, they had to tone down their ideology, radical language, and demands such as an end to Capitalism as this would frighten away new-found allies and donors. The method of co-option is still effective today [similar to past decades] as one way to recruit grassroots activists while depoliticizing their agenda within the neoliberal model.'

Similarly, Kasina critically notes that NGOs are 'dividing the struggle into clusters and getting data and statistics for more funding from the donor community without giving full solutions to the problems communities go through in concrete reality. They want numbers; their fight is not change. Until then, though, shall we continue to document cases in our communities while NGOs are non-political and our issues are political?' The analytical and political no-goes and this-is-too-far-off of many NGOs get also analyzed in the account of Kyaa: The NGO forums she attended some years back never advocated for radical change; most of them were dialogues with local authorities about issues that affected the community. These dialogues did not change anything, really; situations remained the same, and communities continued to suffer. I now see the imperialist ploy; use NGOs to collect data in poor communities for their own records and make sure the community maintains hope rather than fighting for itself to bring permanent radical change, which is socialism.

Against this background, what many authors thus also insist on is that for radical movements, theory and political education - in cells, brigades, homes and communities - are of utmost importance. This, they insist, is to build and deepen political awareness about the economy, society, politics, history, and the terrain of movements and struggles for radical change. It is part of, in Mwangi's words, the 'struggle for ideological autonomy from the state, political parties, and the development apparatus.' This requires also questioning the role of NGOs and of radical movements too, as Kasina emphasizes.

This all is a work in progress, and for some authors in the collection also one of engagement and conversation with some of those who work in NGOs. This, for example, is the end of the text 'disclaimer' in the chapter by Gathanga Ndung'u: 'the reflections therewith are not a vote of doubt to those in the NGO space. It is a self-introspection analysis of the role we should be playing in bringing transformational agendas to the oppressed rather than parading them for study and experimentation programs.' To add, Kasina has this advice to NGOs:

> Going forward, NGOs should try to operate among the people and learn from them, and try to change their material conditions and inspire their revolutionary spirit for change. They should move out of those stakeholder workshops where they discuss poverty reduction strategies and join the working people of Africa in their struggle against oppression. They should be critical of the creation of poverty through the concentration of the means of production in a few hands and the appropriation and subjugation of labor by the bourgeoisie and foreign capital as well as the privatization of social services that is saddled with corruption and bloated bureaucracy. They can show solidarity with trade unions and their attitude should be anti-capitalist and anti-imperialist if they are genuine about the struggle of the suffering people.

This is a timely, important, unique, insightful, not-to-be-missed book. Thank you, comrades, and thank you, Professor Shivji. May the collection find a wide readership, among the young and old, in Kenya and far beyond. And may you find time and energy to turn your analytical-reflective eyes to another important-yet-neglected topic soon. The format you have presented here is a winner.

Leeds, July 2022

# Bibliography

Morefield, Jeanne (2020), When Neoliberalism Hijacked Human Rights. Jacobin.

National Council of NGOs. The National Council of NGOs. (n.d.). Retrieved December 23, 2022, from https://ngocouncilofkenya.org/

Pambazuka News. (n.d.). https://www.pambazuka.org/governance/reflections-ngos-tanzania-what-we-are-what-we-are-not-and-what-we-ought-be

Petras, John (2007), NGOs: In the service of imperialism. Journal of Contemporary Asia. https://doi.org/10.1080/00472339980000221

Washington Post (2017, June 16). Retrieved from https://www.washingtonpost.com/news/monkey-cage/wp/2017/06/16/kenyans-will-vote-in-august-why-are-ngo-government-relations-an-issue

Woods, A. (2017, June 22). Why we are Marxists | Dialectical materialism | History & theory. Retrieved from https://www.bolshevik.info/why-we-are-marxists.htm

Wright. Glen. W. (2012). NGOs and Western hegemony: causes for concern and ideas for change. Development in Practice, Volume 22, Number 1.

# About the Contributors

**Asuwa, Irene** is a community mobilizer and organizer. She is a social scientist with a background on Political Science and Sociology. She co-convenes Ecological Justice and supports outreach at Ukombozi Library.

**Bah, Alieu** is a writer and organizer from the Gambia and a member of Mwamko, a popular political educational collective on the Continent.

**Choto, Tafadzwa Antonater** is a member of the International Socialist Organisation, Zimbabwe Ph.D. candidate of Literature and Philosophy in the Department of Sociology at the University of Johannesburg.

**Gathanga, Samuel** is a biotechnologist, a human rights defender, a researcher, a writer and an ecological and food activist from Mathare Social Justice Centre in Mathare, Nairobi.

**Kaluka, W. Mwaivu** is the National Chairperson of the Young communist League and peasant organiser from Taita Taveta.

**Kamau, Gerald** is a Fighter and Champion for Ecological Environment, Public Spaces and transformation. He is also a Member of Ecological Justice Movement.

**Kasina, Mary Anne** is a writer feminist, a community organizer with the Kayole community Justice center and convener of the women in social justice centers in Kenya.

**Kyaa, Minoo** is a writer, poet and member of Mukuru Community Justice Centre and Team Lead of Social Justice Centers Travelling Theatre. She is also a member of Women in Social Justice Centers movement and a Co-Founder of Just Women-Afrika.

**Maghanga, Lewis** is a member of the Central Committee of the Revolutionary Socialist League, based in Nairobi, Kenya. He is an activist and organizer, and an active participant in the Pan African Movement. He holds a Bachelor's Degree in Economics from the University of Nairobi.

**Mwangi, Nicholas** is a member of the Ukombozi library, the Revolutionary socialist league, the Rastafarian community in Kenya, and co-founder of Dagoretti Social Justice Centre.

**Ndungu, Kinuthia** is a Community Organizer with Kasarani Social Justice Centre and Grassroots Liberation Movement and a member of the Communist Party of Kenya -Young Communist League.

**Njeri, Mary** is a grassroots community organizer, feminist, and an Administrator with MSJC, and organic intellectuals Network.

**Oyoo, Sungu** is a writer and organizer at Kongamano la Mapinduzi.

**Okakah, Rodgers** is the coordinator of Kayole community justice center and member of the Revolutionary socialist league, organic intellectuals Network, Njiru feminists' network, Ecological Justice, and Afrika Youth Movement. He holds a degree in Information Technology.

**Otieno, Ezra** is a writer, and member of the Revolutionary Socialist League and the Organic Intellectuals Network.

**Shivji, Issa G.** is Professor Emeritus of Public Law & First Julius Nyerere Professor of Pan-African Studies, University of Dar es Salaam, Tanzania

**Wanjira, Wanjiru** is a co-founder of Mathare Social Justice Center, host of the liberating minds podcast, and Matigari book club.

**Wiegratz, Jörg** is a Lecturer in Political Economy of Global Development at the School of Politics and International Studies (POLIS), University of Leeds.

# APPENDIX

*I. Silences in NGO Discourse: the Role and Future of NGOs in Africa*

*II. Reflections on NGOs in Tanzania: What We Are, What We Are Not and What We Ought To Be*

Issa G. Shivji

# I

# Silences in NGO discourse: The Role and Future of NGOs in Africa[1]

## Issa G. Shivji

### PREFACE

This paper critically examines the role and future of the NGO in Africa in the light of its self-perception as a non-governmental, non-political, non-partisan, non-ideological, non-academic, non-theoretical, non-profit association of well-intentioned individuals dedicated to changing the world to make it a better place for the poor, marginalized and downcast. The paper argues that the role of NGOs in Africa cannot be understood without clear characterization of the current historical moment.

On a canvas of broad strokes, I depict Africa at the crossroads of the defeat of the national project and the rehabilitation of the imperial project. Faced with an avalanche of diatribes about the 'end of history', I find it necessary, albeit briefly, to reiterate the history of Africa's enslavement: from the first contacts with the Europeans five centuries ago, through the slave trade, to colonialism, and now globalization. The aim of this historical detour is to demonstrate the fundamental antithesis between the national and the imperial projects to identify correctly the place and role of NGOs within them.

I locate the rise, prominence and privileging of the NGO sector in the womb of the neoliberal offensive. Its aims are ideological, economic and political. I argue that NGO discourse, or more correctly: non-discourse, is predicated on the philosophical and political premises of the neoliberal or globalization paradigm. It is in this context that I will discuss the 'five silences', or blind spots, in NGO discourse. I then draw out the implications of these silences for the contemporary and future roles of the NGO sector in Africa.

Before I begin, I must make two confessions. First, my paper is undoubtedly critical, sometimes ruthlessly so, but not cynical. Second,

---

[1] © 2007 Issa G. Shivji

this criticism is also self-criticism since the author has been involved in NGO activism for some fifteen years. Finally, I must make clear that I do not doubt the noble motivations and good intentions of NGO leaders and activists. But we do not judge the outcome of a process by the intentions of its authors. We aim to analyze the objective effects of actions, regardless of their intentions.

## THE NATIONAL PROJECT AND ITS IMPEDIMENTS

### *1885: the Slicing of the African Cake*

By 1885, when European kings, princes and presidents sat in Berlin to slice up the African continent with their geometrical instruments, the African people had already been devastated by the ravages of the West Atlantic slave trade. In West and Central Africa, the indigenous civilizations lay in ruins, from the sophisticated Saharan trade routes with Timbuktu at their center, to the empires of Angola (Davidson 1961). On the Eastern Seaboard, the European invasion, led by the Portuguese, defeated and destroyed the city-states of the Swahili civilization (Davidson 1961) (Sheriff 1987). All in all, some 40,000,000 souls are estimated to have perished in the triangular slave trade, which lasted for roughly four centuries, 1450-1850.

The development of the European and North American industrial revolutions and the global lead this gave to Europe and America was in no small measure built on the back of Africans (Williams 1945). The colonial episode was thus the tail end of long and destructive contact between Europe and Africa. The slave trade tore apart the very social fabric of African societies, destroying their internal processes of change. It imposed on the continent a European worldview in which the peoples of Africa were at the lowest wrung of the so-called civilized order. No other continent, including those that suffered formal European colonization, had its social, cultural and moral order destroyed on this scale.

Dominant European historiography recounts, at best, the colonial episode while ignoring four centuries of precolonial contact. Yet the present cannot be fully understood and grasped, nor the future charted, without constantly keeping in the forefront of our minds the century-old processes cited by Walter Rodney as 'how Europe underdeveloped Africa' (Rodney 1972).

The precolonial and colonial legacy of Africa is a continuing saga of domination, exploitation and humiliation of the continent by European and American imperial powers. My thesis is that this imperial relationship continues, notwithstanding a brief period of nationalism. Below, I briefly recapitulate the salient features of the colonial legacy and the abortive national project.

## The Colonial Legacy

Right from inception, the most important feature of colonialism was the division of the continent into countries and states cutting across 'natural' geographic, cultural, ethnic and economic ties that had evolved historically.

Boundaries were artificially drawn, with rulers literally reflecting the balance of strength and power among the imperial states. The boundaries divided up peoples, cultures, natural resources and historical affinities. Moreover, these newly created countries became subjects of different European powers with their own traditions of political rule, public administration, cultural outlooks, languages and systems of education. Africa was never Africa: it was Anglophone, Francophone, or Lusophone.

Colonial economies answering to the needs and exigencies of metropolitan powers were disintegrated and disarticulated. Notorious export-oriented, vertically-integrated economies based on raw materials exports and the import of manufactured goods were the result. Internal processes of specialization and division of labor with mutual interdependence - craftsmen and cultivators, producers and merchants, industry and agriculture - as possible harbingers of future industrial development were deliberately destroyed and systematically discouraged (Kjekshus 1977, 1996). Within and between countries, development was extremely uneven.

Of course, the underlying economic logic of the colonial economy was the exploitation of natural and human resources. Colonies became sites for generating surplus, while the metropoles were sites of accumulation. The result was the development of the centers and the underdevelopment of the peripheries. Production processes relied heavily on coercion rather than on contractual consensus for reproduction: forced labor, forced peasant production, enforced cash-crop sales, restrictions on organization and association and the criminalization of 'civil relations'. For example, the breach of employment contracts led to penal sanctions, as did the non-cultivation of minimum acreages of cash and food crops. Thus, force was integrated into the process of production (Mamdani 1987) (Shivji 1987, 1998).

People were divided along ethnic, religious and racial lines. Some tribes were labeled martial, therefore, a recruiting ground for soldiers. Others were condemned to be laborers, and their areas became labor reservoirs. Others were supposed to provide political henchmen for the colonial state apparatus. Missionary education became the means by which Christianity would be spread and the souls of pagans saved whilst producing the future educated elite. Indigenous religions and worldviews were condemned as pagans. There was systematic discrimination against Islam, one of the oldest religions to enter and be internalized in Africa.

Existing internal social divisions and stratification of African society were condemned. African were condemned as lazy and indolent, incapable of learning and entrepreneurship. They were to be perpetually ruled and disciplined, suppressed and muted. Meanwhile, traders, craftsmen and skilled labor were imported: South Asians into East Africa, Lebanese into West Africa. Thus, a hierarchy of racial privilege was constructed, the epitome of which was the settler colony. The middle classes that developed in the interstices of the colonized social order were, at best stunted, at worst, caricatures (Fanon 1963).

Religion and education became vehicles for reproducing colonial racial and cultural complexes: white as superior, black as inferior. The white man's beliefs were 'a religion'. The black man's were 'witchcraft' or 'black magic'. The white man's means of communication was language; the black man's was dialect. As Fanon put it:

> The native is declared insensible to ethics; he represents not only the absence of values, but also the negation of values. ... The customs of the colonized people, their traditions, their myths - above all, their myths - are the very sign of that poverty of spirit and of their constitutional depravity. ... The Church in the colonies is the white people's Church, the foreigner's Church. She does not call the native to God's ways but to the ways of the white man, of the master, of the oppressor. And as we know, in this matter many are called but few chosen. (Fanon 1963)

The 'few chosen', the colonized elite, was thus a caricature, alienated from their own people, yet not fully accepted by their master. Sartre sums it up well in his preface to Fanon:

> The European élite undertook to manufacture a native élite. They picked out promising adolescents; they branded them, as with a red-hot iron, with the principles of western culture; they stuffed their mouths full with high-sounding phrases, grand glutinous words that stuck to the teeth. After a short stay in the mother country they were sent home, white-washed. These walking lies had nothing left to say to their brothers; they only echoed. From Paris, from London, from Amsterdam we would utter words 'Parthenon! Brotherhood!' and somewhere in Africa or Asia lips would open '...thenon!...therhood!' It was the golden age. (Sartre, 1963)

The colonial state was an implant, an alien apparatus imposed on the colonized society. It was an excrescence of the metropolitan state without the latter's liberal institutions or politics. It was a despotic state. In the colonial social formation, it did not have its own civil society. So-called civil society was effectively the metropolitan civil society, at best, the narrow European settler community in the colony.

The colonized society was a subject society, a collection of 'heathens' or 'natives', governed by coercion, and regulated by custom. It was not a civil society, constituted by citizens, governed by rights and duties, and regulated by law (Mamdani 1996).

The governance structures of the colonial state reflected and reinforced the racial, ethnic and religious divisions and fragmentations of the colonized society. For the subject society, the policeman, the tax collector and the district commissioner doubling up as a magistrate represented the state, not the legislative councilor or judge. To resolve a dispute with a neighbor, the 'native' went to a chief. To be punished for murder, or non-payment of tax, or theft of a master's property, he was dragged to the magistrate or judge to be imprisoned or hanged.

We may sum up then by stating the obvious. On the eve of independence, African nationalists faced the formidable task of transforming brutalized colonial societies into national societies. The national project thus called for an African revolution in every sense of the word.

## THE NATIONALIST CHALLENGE AND THE DEFEAT OF THE NATIONAL PROJECT

### The First Challenge and Defeat: Pan-Africanism Versus Territorial Nationalism

Colonial divisiveness, both within and between African countries, seriously undermined the national project from its inception. The colonial infrastructure was the exact antithesis of a national economy. The only rationale behind individual African countries as loci of national independence was the fact that each one of them fell under the jurisdiction of a different colonial power. In sum, the colonial rationale became the rationale of the national project: a contradiction in terms and a paradox.

This paradox was acutely felt, if not always clearly understood, by first-generation African nationalists. Tutored in the ways of their European counterparts, African nationalists coined and crafted the demands of their peoples in the European idiom of human rights and national self-determination within an international context, which witnessed a rise of national liberation in the post-war period. Yet, the ideological genesis of African nationalism lay in pan-Africanism. The locus of pan-Africanism was the continent itself, not the artificially created spaces bound by colonial borders called countries.

Literally, therefore, pan-Africanism begat nationalism, rather than the other way round. Pan-Africanism preceded nationalism by almost half a century. Logic and history neatly coincided. The founding fathers of pan-Africanism were African-Americans, the African diaspora, whose identity could only be African, and not Nigerian or Congolese or Kenyan. The leading lights of the independence movement - Kwame Nkrumah, Jomo Kenyatta - were incubated, conceived, propagated and organised in the pan-African movement by the likes of the great George Padmore, W.E.B. DuBois and C. L. R. James (Legum 1965).

When Nkrumah returned to the continent, he envisioned a West African federation rather than an independent Gold Coast. At the threshold of Ghana's independence, Nkrumah, with great foresight, undertook such historical initiatives as the All Africa People's Conferences, bringing together independence parties and trade unions. Leading African nationalists, including Nyerere, realized and repeatedly repeated that there could be no African nationalism without pan-Africanism: 'African nationalism is meaningless, is anachronistic, and is dangerous, if it is not at the same time Pan-Africanism' (Nyerere 1963, 1967).

Nyerere was even prepared to delay the independence of his country to facilitate the East African federation. He argued that once these countries became independent, with their own flags, national anthems, presidents and prime ministers, it would be much more difficult to dissolve individual sovereignties into a larger sovereignty. History proved him right.

Nkrumah constantly and vehemently argued that, left on their own, independent African countries would become pawns on the imperialist chessboard. He, too, was tragically proved right in the case of the Congo. Under the guise of the United Nations, led by the United States, Western imperial powers conspired in the assassination of the great nationalist leader Patrice Lumumba, perpetuating Congo's descent into a cycle of violence, from which it has yet to recover.

As one after another African countries became independent, Nkrumah's All Africa Peoples Conferences dissolved into the Conferences of Independent African States, which eventually formed the Organisation of African Unity (OAU). To the chagrin even of his own friends, Nkrumah continued his battle cry for a union of African states.

Nyerere advocated a gradualist-cum-regional approach to African unity. He clashed with Nkrumah who believed that the regional approach to African unity would, in fact, become an obstacle to the continent's political unity and that regionalism would inevitably play into the hands of imperialism (Shivji 2005). Logic was on the side of Nyerere, but history and political economy proved Nkrumah right.

With great foresight, Nkrumah wrote Neo-Colonialism, the Last Stage of Imperialism, for which imperialism never forgave him. He was overthrown in 1966 by a CIA-sponsored coup. Nyerere's own practical attempt to unite Zanzibar with Tanganyika in 1964 can more accurately be considered a pragmatic response to intense Cold War pressures than an example of pan-African unity (Wilson 1989). The OAU itself was bedeviled by imperial machinations, which led Nyerere, one of its founding fathers, angrily condemning it as a 'trade union of African leaders/states'.

The national project inevitably and inexorably became a statist project. Nationalism resolved itself into various ideologies of developmentalism and nation-building. In the process, it undermined pan-Africanism (Shivji 1986) (Wamba 1991, 1996). Ironically, territorial nationalism became the gravedigger of pan-Africanism, out of which it was born. While paying full tribute to Nkrumah's great vision at the 40th anniversary of Ghana's independence in 1997, Nyerere lamented the failure of first-generation nationalists to unite Africa:

> Once you multiply national anthems, national flags and national passports, seats at the United Nations, and individuals entitled to 21 guns salute, not to speak of a host of ministers, Prime ministers, and envoys, you would have a whole army of powerful people with vested interests in keeping Africa balkanized. (Nyerere 1997)

The second challenge and defeat: the developmental state versus democratic development

The independence movement in Africa was essentially led by the proto-middle classes, or petty bourgeoisie, consisting mostly of educated elite. No doubt it was a mass movement in which Africans were reasserting their Africanness after five centuries of domination and humiliation. Tom Mboya called it 'the rediscovery of Africa by Africans' (Mboya 1963). Amilcar Cabral defined national liberation as the process of 'becoming Africans' (Cabral, 1980). Yet, as some African nationalists had predicted and others painfully realized, territorial nationalism turned out to be an anachronism.

African nationalists, including Nyerere, who took the reins of state at the dawn of independence, had to work within the constraints imposed by territorial nationalism. In the process, they ended up making a virtue of necessity, and the authoritarian logic of the colonial state was reasserted.

The independent state, as Nyerere argued, had the twin tasks of development and nation-building. It preceded the nation (Nyerere 1963). Ironically, however, the state that was supposed to build the nation had inherited the colonial state: it was despotic and divisive, in every respect antithetical to the tasks of nation-building. Nationalism in the hands of the post-colonial state degenerated into statism: politically authoritarian, economically rapacious, internationally compradorial and nationally dictatorial. At best, the ideology of nationalism resolved into various ideologies of developmentalism; at worst, it became ethnicism. The liberal constitutional order that the departing colonial masters bequeathed was a tragic joke because it was superimposed on a despotic apparatus, which had been invented, strengthened and bequeathed by the colonial master. The despotic infrastructure endured while the liberal superstructure blew off into the winds of factional political struggles or so-called development imperatives (Shivji 2003).

'We must run while others walk', Nyerere declared. In the hurry to develop, he added, 'we cannot afford liberal checks and balances'. Justifying the executive or 'imperial' presidency, as it is branded in African jurisprudence, Nyerere wrote in the (London) Observer (Mwaikusa 1995):

> Our constitution differs from the American system in that it ... enables the executive to function without being checked at every turn .... Our need is not for brakes to social change ... - our lack of trained manpower and capital resources, and even our climate, act too effectively already. We need accelerators powerful enough to overcome the inertia bred by poverty, and the resistances which are inherent in all societies.

Independence had raised expectations. To maintain legitimacy, the new regimes had to deliver on both developmental and social fronts. But the colonial state had deliberately suppressed and undermined the development of a middle class, which would have become an agency for development. So, it fell to the state. Regardless of the variety of the ideology, whether capitalist or nominally socialist, the state became a site of private and public accumulation. The public sector played the dominant role in all African countries, from socialist Tanzania to capitalist Malawi. Nyerere justified his program of nationalization more on the grounds of economic nationalism than on the principles of socialism (Nyerere 1968). Whatever the pundits of neoliberalism may proclaim today, the fact remains that the Bretton Woods institutions, together with the so-called 'donor community' and the multinationals, used the African state to serve its own interest while turning a blind eye to mismanagement and corruption.

During the first decade and a half of independence, African economies showed modest growth rates compared to other continents. Nonetheless, they were impressive given the conditions imposed at independence. Investment and savings ranged between 15 to 20 percent of GDP. Primary and secondary school enrolment was expanded. Tertiary education, which in many countries literally did not exist during colonial times, was introduced. Medical and health statistics showed improvement. But this growth and development were unsustainable, as they were predicated on reinforcing colonial foundations.

Growth in agriculture production was based on extensive cultivation rather than a rise in productivity using the industrial processes of fertilization, mechanization and irrigation. It depended heavily on exports of a few primary commodities traded on a hostile and adverse international market. Growth in the manufacturing sector was heavily dependent on import substitution and intermediary inputs, with few internal linkages. The investment was largely public, while private domestic capital was stashed away in foreign countries. According to one estimate, by 1990, 37 percent of Africa's wealth had flown outside the continent (Mkandawire & Soludo 1999). Moreover, foreign capital concentrated in the extractive industries hemorrhaged the economy, rather than contributing to its development.

During this period, the developmental state also borrowed heavily, whether for genuinely productive or prestige projects. Petro-dollars accumulated by international banks during the 1973 oil crisis were offloaded in the form of cheap loans to developing countries. But by the end of the 1970s, cheap loans had turned into heavy debt burdens as the limits of the early growth were reached. The economic shocks of the late 1970s plunged African economies further into deep crises. Numbers fell, growth rates became negative, debt repayments became unsustainable, and fiscal imbalances and inflation were out of control. Social services declined, and infrastructure deteriorated. One after another, African governments - including the radical nationalists - found themselves pleading at the door of the IMF and the Paris club (Campbell & Stein).

Economists have described the 1980s as Africa's lost decade. The 1980s were also a transition period marking the beginnings of the decline of developmentalism and the rise of neoliberalism, euphemistically called globalization. The lost decade signaled both the decline of the developmental state and the loss of its political legitimacy: the loss of both development and democracy. Internally, political stirrings and rethinking began, both practical and ideological.

But as the African political economy has repeatedly demonstrated, the continent is firmly inserted in the imperialist web. Instead of allowing a space to open up for internal popular struggles, the opportunist imperialist intervention derailed it by imposing top-down, so-called multi-party democracy and 'good governance'. Western powers took the opportunity to reassert their political and ideological hegemony. They recovered the ground lost during the nationalist decades, a trajectory worth recapitulating.

## THE THIRD CHALLENGE AND DEFEAT: NATIONALISM VERSUS IMPERIALISM

Colonialism left by the front door and returned through the back door in the form of neocolonialism. Radical nationalists such as Nkrumah and Ben Bella were overthrown in military coups. Lumumba, Pio

Gama Pinto and Thomas Sankara were assassinated in Western sponsored imperial adventures (Blum 1986, 2001) (De Witte 2001). The few who survived including Nyerere and Kaunda did so through compromise and a game of hide-and-seek. Others, for example, Sékou Touré, became paranoid and despotic, apprehensive of being overthrown or assassinated. Others - Kenyatta, Moi, Houphet Boigny and Senghor - became compradors in the bidding of their imperial masters.

Reiterating the need to build nations out of fractious ethnic groups and for rapid development, the post-independence ruling classes and governing elites centralized and concentrated power in the executive arm of the state. On the other hand, they hegemonized autonomous expressions of civil society (Shivji 1991). Elsewhere, ruling factions resorted to whipping up ethnic divisions to retain power.

Yet, it is also true that during this period, imperialism was ideologically on the defensive. The movement of the newly independent countries, principles of non-alignment, UNCTAD, the 'new economic world order', the right to development, the successful Chinese, Cuban, and Nicaraguan revolutions, the defeat of the US in Vietnam, and the worldwide student anti-imperialist movement enhanced the prestige of national liberation movements. This was a period labeled by Samir Amin as 'the period of Bandung excitement' (Amin 1990).

For Africa generally, the triumph of the armed struggles in Mozambique, Angola and Guinea Bissau represented, ironically enough, both the high point of radical nationalism and its precipitous decline in the next decade. Portugal was the weak link in the imperialist chain. It was defeated by the national liberation movement supported by much of the rest of Africa.

But imperialism was not destroyed. The national liberation movement in power had embarked on an alternative, anti-imperialist development path. The struggle between nationalism and imperialism found its most concentrated expression in southern Africa. Imperialism, through its proxy, apartheid South Africa, showed its true colors by supporting terrorist organizations: RENAMO in Mozambique and UNITA in Angola. Such organizations caused havoc leading to compromises on all fronts, change in direction of development and loss of the national liberation vision. The national liberation elites became utterly beholden, disowning their own past, slavishly echoing rising neoliberal rhetoric.

As history will have it, the quasi-success of the South African national liberation movement, one of the longest-standing and most militant, was not the high point in the stand between radical nationalism against imperialism but rather the beginning of its end. By the end of the 1970s and early 1980s, the nationalist era, particularly its territorial variant, was drawing to a close. The defeat of socialism in Eastern Europe and the Soviet Union further narrowed the space for expressing radical nationalism and anti-imperialism.

Imperialism took the offensive, initially on the economic front, with its structural adjustment programs. This was soon followed by an undisguised political and ideological offensive, ridiculing and humiliating nationalism while rehabilitating imperialism. In 1990 Douglas Hurd, the then British Secretary of State, was able to say: 'we are slowly putting behind us a period of history in which the West was unable to express a legitimate interest in the developing world without being accused of "neo-colonialism"' (Furedi 1994). The British historian, John Charmley, launching his book Churchill: The End of Glory could unashamedly declare:

> The British Empire vanishing has had a very deleterious effect on the third world. Look at Uganda under the British and look at it now. And you didn't get famines quite as frequently in Africa then as you do now.

The neoliberal package is and has been more an ideological offensive than simply an economic program. But let us not jump ahead. Instead, I shall retrace the beginnings of the neoliberal phase in Africa.

## THE IMPERIAL PROJECT AND ITS SUCCOURS

### The Neoliberal Offensive

The imperialist offensive came on the heel of the defeat of the national project to destroy and bury it. This was, by definition, the immanent dream of imperialism. On the economic front, the neoliberal package boils down to further deepening the integration of African economies in the world capitalist system, thus reproducing essentially colonial and neocolonial economic structures.

In 1981 the World Bank published its notorious report, Accelerated Development for Africa: an Agenda for Africa. It certainly was an agenda for Africa, set by the erstwhile Bretton Woods institutions (BWIs) with the backing of Western countries. But it had little to do with development, accelerated or otherwise. The report and subsequent structural adjustment programs concentrated on stabilizing measures: eliminating budget deficits, bringing down inflation rates, getting prices right, unleashing the free market and liberalizing trade.

According to the World Bank, the villain of the declining economic performance in Africa was the state: it was corrupt and dictatorial, with no capacity to manage the economy and allocate resources rationally. It was bloated with bureaucracy; its mode of operation was nepotism. The BWIs refused to bail out the crisis-ridden economies unless the governments adopted structural adjustment programs that ensured stabilizing the fundamentals.

Balancing budgets involved cutting agricultural subsidies and spending on social programs including education and health. Unleashing the free market meant doing away with the protection of infant industries and rolling back the state in economic activity. The results of structural adjustment have been devastating, as many studies have shown. Social indicators show that education, medical care, health, nutrition, rates of literacy and life expectancy have all declined. De-industrialization and redundancies have ensued. Even some of the most modest achievements of the nationalist or developmentalist period were lost or undermined (Gibbon 1993, 1995) (Adedeji 1993).

As the international situation changed with the collapse of the Soviet Union, Western imperialist powers regained the ideological initiative. The neoliberal package of marketisation, privatization and liberalization became the policy for (but not of) African states. Good performers were praised and rewarded with more aid while the insubordinate and recalcitrant were parodied, left to their own resources. Whilst aid had always come with strings, there was no longer any attempt to disguise it.

Political conditionalities - multi-party democracy, good governance, human rights etc. - were added to economic conditionalities. Decision-making and policymaking slipped out of the hands of African states as the West financed policy and governance consultants in their thousands to produce policy blueprints, poverty reduction strategies and manuals on good governance. This absorbed some US$4 billion annually. In 1985, to give just one example, foreign experts resident in Equatorial Guinea were paid three times the total government public sector wage bill (Mkandawire & Soludo 1999).

National liberation ideologies have been rubbished, and national self-determination declared passé. Africa is told it has only one choice: integrate fully into the globalized world or remain marginalized. The specter of marginalization is so rampant that even progressive African scholars dare say that 'Africa may be graduating from being the region with "lost development decades" to becoming the world's forgotten continent' (Mkandawire & Soludo).

The former US ambassador to Tanzania, my country, speaking to lawmakers, was blatant about what the superpower expected of African states:

> The liberation diplomacy of the past, when alliances with socialist
> nations were paramount, and so-called Third World Solidarity
> dominated foreign policy, must give way to a more realistic
> approach to dealing with your true friends - those who are working

to lift you into the twenty-first century, where poverty is not
acceptable, and disease must be conquered.[2]

African leaders are left with little options: 'you are either with
globalization or doomed!' They have fallen into line, one after
another, even if it has meant disowning their own past. The report of
Tony Blair's Commission for Africa, which consisted of prominent
Africans, including one president and one prime minister, castigates
the last three decades in entirety - which virtually means the whole of
the post-independence period - as 'lost decades' (Graham 2005). The
primary responsibility for bad governance and lack of accountability
is placed on the African state. The report totally ignores the role of
imperialism in both the exploitation of African resources and in
lending support to non-democratic states when it suited their
interests. Africans are told they have no capacity to think. African
states are told they have no capacity to formulate correct policies. As
the commission declared - with a straight face:

> Africa's history over the last fifty years has been blighted by two
> areas of weakness. These have been capacity - the ability to design
> and deliver policies; and accountability - how well a state answers to
> its people.  (emphasis in the original)

So, policymaking, an important aspect of sovereignty, has been
wrenched out of the hands of the African state, which is placed on the
same level as other so-called stakeholders, including NGOs.

## THE FUNDAMENTAL PREMISES OF GLOBALIZATION OR NEOLIBERALISM

Globalization in Africa is manifest in the neoliberal economic and
political packages, centering around trade liberalization, privatization
of national assets and resources, the commodification of social
services and marketization of goods and services, both tangible and
intangible.

In sum, the underlying thrust of neoliberal and globalized
development 'discourse' is for deeper integration of African
economies into global capital and market circuits without
fundamental transformation. It is predicated on private capital, which
in Africa translates into foreign private capital, as the 'engine of
growth'. It centers on economic growth without questioning whether
growth necessarily translates into development.

It banishes issues of equality and equity to the realm of rights
rather than development. And 'rights' are reduced to the purview of
advocacy NGOs, no longer a terrain for popular struggle. 'Human-

---

[2] Press Release, U.S. Embassy in Tanzania, 29 July, 2003.

centered' or 'people-driven' development approaches, previously the kingpins of African alternatives, such as the Lagos Plan of Action, are pooh-poohed into non-existence. The development falls within the purview of development practitioners and development NGOs, which advocate right-based development.

The African people, who were once supposed to be the authors and drivers of development and liberators of their nations, are reduced to the category of 'the chronically poor'. They become the subject matter of poverty reduction strategy papers authored by consultants and discussed at stakeholder workshops in which the 'poor' are represented by NGOs. The 'poor': the diseased, the disabled, the Aids-infected, the ignorant, the marginalized, in short, the 'people', are not part of the development equation since development is assigned to the private capital that constitutes the 'engine of growth'. The 'poor' are the recipients of humanitarian aid provided by 'true friends', (thanks to the American ambassador for that phraseology), dispensed by non-partisan, non-political, presumably non-involved, non-governmental organizations. In these societies, where stakeholders never tire of policymaking for the poor, its twin opposite - the rich – does not appear to exist. It is said that these societies consist only of the poor and the wealth creators, not of producers and appropriators of wealth.

In this neoliberal discourse, the African state is cast as the villain. African bureaucracies are demonized as corrupt, incapable and unable to learn. Thus, they need globalized foreign advisors and consultants, now termed development practitioners, to mentor, monitor and oversee them. Among the mentors and monitors are of course, the NGOs. The so-called advisors and consultants move freely between the triad family consisting of the 'DONs' (donor organizations), the 'INFOs' (international financial organizations) and the NGOs, including 'GoNGOs' (government-organized NGOs) and the 'DoNGOs' (donor-organized NGOs).

In this 'discourse' the developmental role of the state is declared dead and buried. Instead, it is assigned the role of 'chief' to supervise the globalization project under the tutelage of imperial - now called development - partners or 'true friends'. The irony of the recent British Commission for Africa was that it was convened, constituted and chaired by a British prime minister, while an African president and a prime minister sat on it as members. This symbolizes the nature of the so-called 'new partnership'. The message is clear: African 'copartners' in African development are neither equal nor in the driving seat.3

It is true that the neoliberal discourse has not gone without challenge, both intellectual and practical. African people have fought on the streets against structural adjustment policies. They have protested in their villages, towns and neighborhoods. African intellectuals have written and argued to illustrate the fallacy of the underlying assumptions of neoliberalism and globalisation.

Yet, it is also true, at least for the time being, that neoliberalism is holding sway. Virtually the whole of the African political elite and establishment has fallen into line, (unlike, for example, in Latin America), whether for pragmatic reasons of survival or else to defend their own vested interests. A large part of the African intellectual elite has been co-opted and accommodated within the neoliberal discourse.

This paper argues that the sudden rise of NGOs and their apparently prominent role in Africa are part of this neoliberal, organizational and ideological offensive.

## NGOS OR THE SO-CALLED 'THIRD SECTOR'

At the inception of the neoliberal offensive in the early 1980s, the rise and role of NGOs were explained and justified within the conceptual framework of the problematic of civil society. The concept of civil society came into vogue in the 1980s, during the collapse of the Soviet and East European systems, and the democratization drive in Africa. In Eastern Europe, following the collapse of bureaucratic socialist regimes (or actually existing socialism, as they were then christened), the construction of civil societies was seen as returning to 'normal society on the Western model'. In Eastern Europe itself, the term has been used in as many different ways as contexts (Shivji 2002).

Civil society discourse in Africa has too used the term with all kinds of meanings: from associational connotations - 'civil societies', to all-virtuous, harmonious social spaces. But it is in the meaning of free associations, 'independent' of the state, that the term has stuck. Very often the term 'civil society organization' (CSO) is used interchangeably with NGO.

Influenced heavily, as always, by US-based Africanists, a false bipolarity or dichotomy between state and civil society has predominated. Within neoliberal ideologies, the state is demonized.

---

3 The irony of Blair's Africa Commission turns cynical when it is recalled that one of Blair's commissioners, President Mkapa, comes from the same country whose first President, Nyerere, in retirement, chaired the South Commission which was conceived and financed by the South!

ISSA G. SHIVJI

Civil society, often conflated with NGOs, is privileged. NGOs are presented as the 'third sector', the other two sectors being the state - power, politics, and the private sector - capital, economics. This ideological presentation of NGOs also dominates self-perception in the NGO world itself. Yet it is based on utterly false historical and intellectual premises and posits serious political implications (Shivji 2002).

The concept of civil society in European history represented the transition from a medieval feudalist to a capitalist society. This was part of the bourgeois revolution. In that context, civil society was, for both Hegel and Marx and perhaps even for Weber, an ensemble of free, equal and abstract individuals associating in the public sphere of production as opposed to the private sphere of the family. For Marx, civil society was synonymous with bourgeois society. The concept is developed in opposition to feudal relations where the public and the private are merged, and statuses are determined by birth and privileges and where politics is direct, 'that is to say, the elements of civil life, for example, property, or the family, or the mode of labor were raised to the level of political life in the form of seignority, estates, and corporations'. (Sayers 1991)

At the same time for Marx - and this is directly relevant to our conceptual debate about civil society - whereas civil society presents itself as an ensemble of free individuals and as a separate sphere from the state or politics, it is in fact the soil from which state power arises, and in which it is embedded. For our purpose, it is necessary to highlight two conclusions. First, the so-called civil society, in the sense of the public sphere of production, is not a harmonious whole; rather a terrain of contradictory relations between classes – the two poles being the producer class and the appropriator class. Second, the separation between state and civil society, between economics and politics, is ideological. It is how the bourgeois society appears and presents itself. In reality, those who command and control the sphere of production also wield political power – that is the state.

When applied to colonial society, we find that the colonial sphere of production is essentially controlled by imperial capital. The colonial mode of production is characterized by the extraction of surplus from non-capitalist classes through the use of state force. The national bourgeois project promised by the independence movement is aborted and defeated. In the 1960s and 1970s, there was a great debate among Third World intellectuals as to whether a national bourgeois project could ever succeed in the Third World, particularly in Africa, in an era of imperialism (Amin 1990) (Tandon 1982) (Mahjoub 1990).

Be that as it may, the transformation from a colonial subject society to a bourgeois civil society in Africa is incomplete, stunted and distorted. We have the continued domination of imperialism –

reproduction of the colonial mode – in a different form, currently labelled globalization or neoliberalism. Within this context, NGOs are neither a third sector nor independent of the state. Rather they are inextricably imbricated in the neoliberal offensive, which follows on the heels of the crisis of the national project. Unless there is awareness on the part of the NGOs of this fundamental moment in the struggle between imperialism and nationalism, they end up playing the role of ideological and organizational foot soldiers of imperialism, however, this is described.

Below, I demonstrate how five silences in the NGO discourse contribute to the mystification and obfuscation of the role of NGOs.

## THE FIVE SILENCES

### *What Are NGOs?*

To preface this section, I provide a quick factual summary of the salient features of NGOs in the African setting.

Firstly, many African NGOs were born in the womb of the neoliberal offensive, which began to open up space for freedom of association. One feature of the statist period was the organizational hegemony of the state. In the first flush of the opening up of organizational space, NGOs proliferated without critical examination of the place and role of NGOs and their underlying ideologies and premises. The anti-state stance of the so-called donor community was the real push behind the upsurge in NGO activity.

Secondly, NGOs are led by and largely composed of the educated elite. They are located in urban areas and well-versed in the language and idiom of modernization. Broadly three types of NGO elites may be identified.

The first category is the radical elite that was previously involved in political struggles, with an explicit vision for change and transformation, but which found itself suppressed under the statist hegemony. Many of these elites took the opportunity to express themselves politically in the NGOs. They saw NGOs as a possible terrain of struggle for change. This section of the elite is politically motivated, without being necessarily involved in partisan party-politics.

The second category includes well-intentioned individuals driven by altruistic motives to improve the conditions of their fellow human beings and compatriots. In other words, they are morally motivated.

The third category is the mainstream elite, not infrequently former government bureaucrats, who shifted to the NGO world once they found that donor funding was being directed there. The motivation of this elite is simply careerist. It is driven by material gains rather than altruism. It is personally motivated. This category keeps swelling as jobs in the state and private sector become more and more competitive or difficult to come by.

Thirdly, an overwhelming number of NGOs are donor funded. They do not have any independent source of funding. They have to seek donor funds through customary procedures set by the funding agencies. In this respect, the degree of independence they can exercise in relation to donor agenda varies from NGO to NGO, depending on the perspectives of its leadership. In practice, though, as would be readily acknowledged by even the most radical among them, their scope for action is limited.

This does not necessarily mean that a few may not exercise greater autonomy in their outlook and ideology and still be accepted; exceptions are necessary to prove the rule.

While some NGOs may be quite involved with and appreciated by the people whom they purport to serve, ultimately, NGOs, by their very nature, derive not only their sustenance but also their legitimacy from the donor community. In the current international conjuncture, even political elites located in the state or political parties seek legitimacy from so-called 'development partners', rather than from their own people. Not surprisingly, there is a fair amount of elite circulation between government and non-governmental sectors.

Fourthly, by far the greatest number of NGOs are advocacy NGOs focusing on particular areas of activity such as human rights, gender, development, environment and governance. There are always NGOs set up by politically or morally motivated individuals with a genuine desire to 'do something', and who are genuinely meant to respond to the need of the people. But it is also true that a substantial number of NGOs are set up to respond to whatever is perceived to be in vogue among the donor community at any particular time. Donor-driven NGOs, I would guess, are perhaps the most dominant.

Besides advocacy tasks, NGOs are also increasingly commissioned by donors, or the state or even the corporate sector, to undertake consultancy work or be their executive agencies to dispense funds or services. Thus, NGOs have come to play a major role in the aid industry. In the NGO world, it is not at all ironic that a non-governmental body is assigned by the government to do a governmental job and is funded by a donor agency, which in turn is an outfit of a foreign government. Thus, USAID may fund a gender NGO to raise awareness among women about a new land law whose terms of reference are set by a government ministry. To complete the picture, one may find that the same USAID may have recommended and sponsored a consultant who drafted the land law for the government in the first place.

Fifth, while most NGOs may insert in their charters a vision or mission statement, these are often vague, amorphous and meaningless – for example, 'poverty-reduction'. In any case, they are quickly forgotten. What takes over are the so-called strategic plans and log-frames, which can be tabulated, quantified and ticked for triennium reports and proposals for more funding. The 'success' of an NGO is measured by how efficiently it is managed and run. The criteria for measuring efficiency are borrowed from the corporate sector. Training NGOs are set up to train NGO managers in 'strategic framework analysis', in charting 'inputs' and 'outcomes' tables, in setting indicators and in methods and techniques to log the vision and the mission and the strategy in log-frames. As Brian Murphy observes (Murphy 2001):

> This ethos has been embraced by and is now aggressively - sometimes ruthlessly - promoted by senior managers in many of our leading NGOs, convinced that restructuring our organisations along corporate lines is the ticket to successful integration in the new trilateral global order that sees the public, private, and voluntary sectors somehow as partners in development. ... Increasingly the model for the 'successful' NGO is the corporation - ideally a transnational corporation and NGOs are ever more marketed and judged against corporate ideals. As part of the trend, a new development scientism is strangling us with things like strategic framework analysis and results-based management, precisely the values and methods and techniques that have made the world what it is today.

Below, I illustrate how the rise, role and features of NGOs, which objectively situate them within the imperial project, are reinforced by certain 'silences' in NGO discourse.

## PRIVILEGING ACTIVISM OR CHANGING THE WORLD WITHOUT UNDERSTANDING IT

During the revolutionary moment of the 1960s and 1970s, when the national liberation movement was at its height, it used to be said that we should 'think globally and act locally'. This summed up four fundamental ideas. One, imperialism was global and oppressed all peoples worldwide. So it must be understood in its global context. Two, imperialism would have to be fought at the level of its local manifestations. The concrete analysis of the concrete situation was underlined. Three, the slogan expressed the international solidarity of all peoples across the globe against imperialism. Four, imperialism had to be clearly understood and correctly described in all aspects to conduct an organized and conscious struggle against it.

These assumptions informed the basis of profound intellectual debates on the theory and practice of imperialism and national liberation. As Amilcar Cabral, one of the foremost leaders of the African liberation movement put it: 'every practice produces a theory...if it is true that a revolution can fail even though it be based on perfectly conceived theories, nobody has yet made a successful revolution without a revolutionary theory' (Cabral 1969).

What is interesting about that period is that radical intellectual discourse was integrated with militant activism; the two were mutually reinforcing. The NGO discourse in the current period of apparent imperial 'triumphalism' eschews theory and emphasizes and privileges activism. In the African setting, in particular, whatever is left of critical intellectual discourse, largely located in the universities, runs parallel to and is divorced from NGO activism. The requirements of funding agencies subtly discourage, if not exhibit outright hostility to a historical, social and theoretical understanding of development, poverty and discrimination. Our erstwhile benefactors now tell us: 'just act, don't think'; and we shall fund both.

The inherent bias against theory is manifested at various levels. I will mention a couple. First, the penchant for project funding, which is supposed to be operated and completed within a given time – triennium, for example, does not admit thinking about the underlying premises of the so-called project. The managerial techniques of monitoring and evaluating projects through log-frames, by their very nature, compartmentalize and dissect life to such an extent that the sight of the whole, even the capacity to think holistically, is lost.

Secondly, the projects are issue-based and are supposed to be addressed as issues. The issue itself is identified as a problem at the level of phenomenon; its underlying basis needs to be addressed but assumed. The issue is isolated and abstracted from its social, economic and historical reality; therefore, its interconnectedness to other issues and the whole is lost.

Thirdly, issue-oriented and time-limited projects only allow for long-term basic research based on solid theoretical and historical premises. So-called research by NGOs or consultants (rather than researchers), if it relates to anything at all, relates to policy and not to the social, economic and political interests underlying the phenomenon under investigation. Nor does it relate to how these interests reproduce themselves. Thus 'research' by consultants degenerates into rapid appraisals, not much more than opinion polls.

In sum, NGO activism is presented and based on the 'act now, think later' mantra. Theory, and particularly grand theory, is dismissed as academicism, unworthy of activists. Yet, we know, that every practice gives rise to theory and that every action is based on some theoretical or philosophical premise or outlook. NGO action is also based on certain theoretical premises and philosophical outlooks. In their case however, theory is written off as 'common sense' and therefore not interrogated.

I believe I have shown sufficiently that the 'common sense' theoretical assumption of the current period underpinning NGO roles and actions is neoliberalism in the interest of global imperialism. It is fundamentally contrary to the interests of the large majority of the people. Taking for granted the fundamentals of neoliberalism and financial capitalism, or challenging them only piece-meal on specific issues, for example, debt, environment or gender discrimination, actually draws the NGOs as protagonists into the imperial project. Brian Murphy argues that many mainstream NGO leaders have internalized assumptions and ways of neo-conservatism and are convinced that globalization akin to neoliberalism is inevitable and irreversible. Thus, they have joined 'its acolytes, ironically without much critical analysis of what "it" actually is or means'. He continues: 'What the corporate PR manager understands implicitly as economic propaganda, NGO people often repeat as articles of faith' (Murphy 2001).

## *The Permanent Present*

Of late, African poverty has been brought to the center stage of the NGO world, ironically by the likes of imperial leaders such as Tony Blair. The African NGO world echoes and repeats the slogan generated by their Northern benefactors: 'Make Poverty History'. But how can you make poverty history without understanding the history of poverty? We need to know how the poverty of the five billion of this world came about. Even more acutely, we need to know how the filthy wealth of the 500 multinationals or the 225 richest people was created (Peacock 2002). We need to know precisely how this great divide, this unbridgeable chasm, is maintained. How it reproduced itself, and it is increasingly deepened and widened. We need to ask ourselves: What are the political, social, moral, ideological, economic and cultural mechanisms which produce, reinforce and make such a world not only possible but seemingly acceptable?

Yet, the NGO discourse seems to have internalized the thoughtless idiocies of right-wing reactionary writers such as Francis Fukuyama, who propagate the 'end of history' in which the present – that is, of course, the present global capitalism under the hegemony of the imperialist North – is declared permanent. Any historical understanding of our present state is ridiculed and dismissed or tolerated as a token to create the illusion of 'diversity'. In the African setting, any discussion of colonial history invariably elicits the standard response: stop blaming the colonialists. How long shall we continue lamenting colonialism? Thus, history is reduced to a blaming exercise and ridiculed.

However, as I have sketched out, colonial and imperial history is at the heart of the present African condition. History is not about assigning or sharing the blame. Nor it is about narrating the 'past', which must be forgotten and forgiven, or remembered once a year on remembrance of heroes or independence days. History is about the present. We must understand the present as history so as to change it for the better, per force, in the African context where the imperial project is not only historical but the lived present. Just as we cannot 'make poverty history' without understanding the history of poverty, so we cannot chant 'another world is possible' without accurately understanding and correctly describing the existing world of five billion slaves and 200 slave masters. How did it come about, and how does it continue to exist? Indeed, to answer these questions, we must understand history as the philosophy and political economy that underpin the existing world and the vested interests – real social interests of real people - that ensure and defend its existence.

## Society as a Harmonious Whole of Stakeholders

Much of the NGO discourse is based on the following premises, inherent in the liberal capitalist world outlook and its new globalization variant. First, the separation of self and society, where society is seen as an aggregate sum of atomic individuals. Second, the liberal goal is to privilege individual interests which are knowable and ascertainable (individual self-determination in the language of post-modernism), assuming that social interests would thus have been taken care of. In the post-modernist variant, social interests are, in any case, unknowable. Third, the social whole is presented as a harmonious whole in which there is a range of more or less equal but diverse interests. The premise that social interests are not all at the same level, that some are dominant and in conflict with others, is eschewed.

The neoliberal model of development based on private property and accumulation, the market as the motor of society, and commodification of resources, services and basic needs is taken as 'common sense', requiring no further proof. In Africa, this translates into further and deeper integration of economies into the global capital and market circuits; the opening up of natural wealth and resources for the exploitation of voracious transnational corporations; and outlawing resistance as at best, aberrant or outdated, at worst, 'terrorist'.

Thus is derived the basis of the so-called triad of stakeholders – the state, the private sector and the voluntary sector. The state is presented as the neutral referee, the guarantor of law and order, whose main function is to provide stability and an enabling environment for the private capital. Private capital is the main engine or motor of growth, which will eventually trickle down to the whole of society. In this drive for inexorable growth and progress, it is acknowledged that some will inevitably be left behind, marginalized, or simply unable to cope: the so-called poor.

Therefore the voluntary sector is needed to take care of them. Social welfare and the provision of basic needs and services to the community are no longer the responsibility of the state or the private sector; instead, they are assigned to NGOs. Thus the 'holy trinity' of development partners is completed: state, capital and NGOs, the latter supposedly the major stakeholders in participatory development enterprise.

The net effect is the legitimization of the essentially exploitative capitalist system presented as pro-poor and morally driven by the so-called NGO sector. The progressive agenda of people-driven development - the radical, populist agenda of the nationalists of yesteryear - is co-opted. In effect, therefore, we see a re-enactment of the missionary positions of the colonial time where church, charity and catechists played the legitimizing role in the colonial enterprise, duping the colonized and damning the freedom fighters. The role assigned to NGOs is in principle not very different, whatever the secular, universal and globalized platitudes are in which it is articulated: 'global neighborhood', 'global village', 'global citizenship'. (Manji & O'Coill 2002) Just as the colonial enterprise assumed the garb of a civilizing mission and used the church as its avant-garde, so the globalization pundits speak the language of secular human rights, using the NGOs as their ideological foot soldiers.

The international and national orders within which we are functioning are unequal and conflicting interests exist. To pretend that society is a harmonious whole of stakeholders is to be complicit in perpetuating the status quo in the interest of the dominant classes and powers. In the struggle between national liberation and imperialist domination and between social emancipation and capitalist slavery, NGOs have to choose sides. In this, there are no in-betweens.

### Non-Governmental Equals Non-Political?

The separation between politics and economics, between state and civil society is how the bourgeois society appears and presents itself. But it is not its real essence. In reality, politics is the quintessence, or the concentrated form of economics. The political sphere is built on the sphere of production, and there is a close relationship between those who command production and those who wield power. Yet the NGO sector, which according to its own proclamations, stands for change, accepts the ideological myth that it is the third sector: non-political, non-profit, having nothing to do with power or production. This bourgeois mythology mystifies the reality of capitalist production and power, thus contributing to its legitimization. NGOs, by accepting the myth of being non-political, contribute to the process of mystification and, therefore, objectively side with the status quo, contrary to their expressed stand for change.

Ironically, non-political NGOs are involved in the process of so-called policymaking. They participate in or are made to feel that they participate in, policymaking and policy dialogue among stakeholders. This has several implications. First, policymaking, an attribute of sovereignty for which the government of the day and supposedly accountable to its people, is wrenched from the state and vested in the amorphous coterie of 'development partners' or stakeholders. Everyone knows who the determining stakeholder really is. The old adage applies: he who pays the piper calls the tune.

Second, the notion that NGOs really participate in policymaking is an illusion. In this day and age of donor-driven policies, this applies equally to the African state itself. Thirdly, it is presumptuous on the part of NGOs to pretend that they represent the people in the policymaking process. Fourthly, the whole process undermines the supposedly democratic and representative character of the state. As the state abdicates responsibility for 'its' policies, ceasing to be accountable to its own people, it becomes accountable instead to the so-called development partners.

Finally, the process of policymaking, a political process par excellence, is presented as if it were a neutral non-political exercise in which non-political NGOs may participate without losing non-partisanship. Needless to say, policymaking is a terrain of intense conflicts of interest and has nothing neutral about it. The question is, as always, which interest is being served by a particular policy. A question about which there can be neither neutrality nor non-partisanship.

## What Is a Better or Alternative World?

'A better world is possible' according to the NGO slogan. But to build a better world, we must understand the world better. This, then, is my message. 'An alternative world is possible' is another adage of the NGOs. But the underlying question remains: what would such an alternative world in the current African context look like? I have tried to argue that Africa is at the crossroads of the defeat of the national project and the reassertion of the imperial project. The national liberation struggles of the 1960s and 1970s, which put imperialism on the ideological defensive, have been aborted. Imperialism by the name of globalization is returning while refurbishing its moral and ideological image. Or at least it is in the process of refurbishing its image. NGOs were born in the womb of neoliberalism and knowingly or otherwise are participating in the imperial project.

There is little doubt that there are very fine and dedicated people in the NGOs, genuinely committed to the struggle for a better world. But there are serious blind spots and silences in NGO discourse, which objectively result in the NGO world participating in the imperial rather than in the national project. NGOs cannot be pro-people and pro-change without being anti-imperialist and anti-status quo.

Arguably, NGOs must engage in critical discourse and political activism rather than assume false neutrality and non-partisanship. In this perspective, African NGOs need to build bridges with African intellectuals and scholars where there is a serious debate, albeit on the fringes of the mainstream, about the 'alternative African world'. Currently, under another false dichotomy between activism and intellectualism, critical intellectual discourse runs parallel to NGO discourse. We need, therefore, to bring together African activism and African intellectualism in a dialogue that critically interrogates both 'our' comprador states and their imperial masters.

## CONCLUSION

To conclude, I will briefly sketch some of the thinking that is emerging among critical scholarship in Africa.

### *Towards Pan-African Liberation, Social Justice and Human Emancipation: Where Do We Stand?*

We must first record that the neoliberal project in Africa has not simply been accepted without practical and intellectual resistance. In a preface to a book by African scholars significantly subtitled Beyond Dispossession and Dependence, Nyerere observed:

> 'Africa's history is not only one of slavery, exploitation and colonialism; it is also a story of struggle against these evils, and of battles won after many setbacks and much suffering.' (Adedeji 1993)

Just as the African people have struggled and opposed structural adjustment in the streets, African intellectuals have critically scrutinized its neoliberal underpinnings and exposed globalization as a new form of imperialism. African NGOs must creatively appropriate these intellectual insights. They must learn from the actually existing struggles of the people before evangelizing awareness-raising of donor-fads of the day: gender, human rights, female genital mutilation, good governance, etc. The educators must first be educated.

Secondly, critically interrogating the national project, African scholars have noted the resurgence of nationalism and observed both its positive and negative aspects. The first lesson is that the African national project located at the territorial level is bound to fail. African nationalism, as some of the fathers of African nationalism realized, is and must be pan-African. Pan-Africanism, they argue, is the nationalism of the era of globalization; and only pan-Africanism can carry forward the struggle for national liberation in Africa. Without a pan-African vision, there is the danger that the resurgence of nationalism as a reaction to the new imperial assault could degenerate into narrow, parochial, nationalist chauvinism, even ethnicism and racism (Shivji 2005) (Yieke 2005).

But this new pan-Africanism must be a bottom-up people's pan-Africanism, and not a top-down statist pan-Africanism. In the hands of the African state and its 'leaders', pan-Africanism will degenerate into 'NEPAD-ism', or phony African renaissance (Landsberg & Kornegey 1998). The New Partnership for African Development (NEPAD), as the name itself suggests, is a donor-dependent program seeking more aid and assistance from the erstwhile 'international community', predicated on further integration of Africa into unequal global structures (Nyong'o et. al 2002). A 'feudo-imperial partnership', the objective of NEPAD is 'for the African canoe to be firmly tied to the North's neoliberal ship on the waters of globalisation', according to Adebayo Adedeji (Nyong'o, 2002).

Thirdly, a fundamental transformation of African societies - an African revolution if you like - is very much on the agenda. The nature of this revolution is very much debated. It is suggested though that it must be a revolution that is thoroughly anti-imperialist and consistently pro-people: a revolution based on popular power, fighting for and defending popular livelihoods, predicated on popular participation (Mafeje 2002) (Shivji 2000).

Fourthly, actually existing states in Africa are essentially compradorised; that is, they are neither democratic nor pro-people. States themselves must be restructured and reorganized with roots in the people and seeking legitimacy from the people rather than from a consortia of G8 ('the global gobblers') imperial powers otherwise known as the 'international community'.

Fifthly, the African people must recover their sovereignty and self-determination: their right to think for themselves and in genuine solidarity with the oppressed people of the world.

Above all, there is a need to integrate intellectual and activist discourse. Only then can NGOs truly play the role of catalysts of change rather than catechists of aid and charity. Indeed, the potential of the NGO sector to play such a role has been demonstrated, albeit in infancy, in such struggles as the Seattle street fights against the world's foremost imperial institutions and the demonstrations condemning the invasion of Iraq against the world's foremost and most brutal superpower.

If NGOs are to play that role, they must fundamentally re-examine their silences and their discourses. They must scrutinize the philosophical and political premises that underpin their activities. They must investigate the credentials of their development partners and the motives of their financial benefactors. They must distance themselves from oppressive African states and comprador ruling elites. NGOs must refuse to legitimize, rationalize and provide a veneer of respectability and morality for global pillage carried out by voracious transnationals under the tagline of 'creating a global village'.

Because I dare say that if we in the NGO world did understand the history of poverty and enslavement in Africa, if we did scrutinize the credentials of so-called development partners, if we did distance ourselves from the oppressive African state, if we did refuse to lend our names to poverty reduction policies and strategies, meant to legitimize the filthy rich; if indeed, we vowed to be catalysts of change and refused to be catechist of charity, we would have been toyi-toyi-ing at the doorsteps of Blair and his commissioners, beating our tom-toms and singing 'make imperialism history' instead of jumping on the bandwagon of Sir Bob Geldof's Band Aid.

## REFERENCES

Adedeji, A., ed. 1993, *Africa within the World: Beyond Dispossession and Dependence*, London: Zed

Amin, S., 1990, *Maldevelopment: Anatomy of a Global Failure*, London: Zed

Blum, W., 1986, T*he CIA, a Forgotten History*, London: Zed

Blum, W., 2001, *Rogue State, A Guide to the World's Only Superpower*, London: Zed

Bond, P., ed. 2002, *Fanon's Warning: a Civil Society Reader on the New Partnership for Africa's Development*, New Jersey: Africa World Press

Cabral, A., 1969, 'The weapon of theory', in Amilcar Cabral, *Revolution in Guinea*, London: Stage 1

Cabral, A., 1980, *Unity and Struggle: Speeches and Writings*, London: Heinemann

Campbell, H., & H. Stein, eds., 1991, *The IMF and Tanzania*, Harare: SAPES

Davidson, B., 1961, *Black Mother: A Study of the Precolonial connection between Africa and Europe*, London: Longman

De Witte, L, 2001, *The Assassination of Lumumba*, Johannesburg: Jacana

Fanon, F., 1963, *The Wretched of the Earth*, London: Penguin

Furedi, F., 1994, *The New Ideology of Imperialism*, London: Pluto Press

Graham, Y., 2005, 'Africa's second 'last chance'', Red Pepper/G8 Africa Commission, http://www.redpepper.org.uk/global/x-jul05-graham.htm

Himmelstrand, U. et. al. eds., 1994, *African Perspectives on Development*, London: James Currey

Kjekshus, H., 1977 & 1996, *Ecology Control and Economic Development in East African History*, London: James Curry

Landsberg, C. & F. Kornegey, 1998, 'The African Renaissance: a quest for Pax Africana and Pan-Africanism', in *Foundation for Global Dialogue,* South Africa and Africa: Reflections on the African Renaissance, FGD Occasional paper No. 17

Legum, L., 1965, *Pan-Africanism: A Short Political Guide*, (Revised edition) London: Pall Mall Press

Mafeje, A., 2002, 'Democratic governance and new democracy in Africa: Agenda for the Future', in Nyong'o, Ghirmazion & Lamba, eds. 2002, *New Partnership for Africa's Development, NEPAD: A New Path?* Nairobi: Heinrich Boll Foundation

Mahjoub, A., 1990, *Adjustment or De-linking?* London: Zed/UNU

Mamdani, M., 1987, 'Contradictory class perspectives on the question of democracy', in Peter Anyang' Nyongo, ed., *Popular Struggles for Democracy in Africa*, London: United Nations University/Zed

Mamdani, M., 1996, *Citizen and Subject: Contemporary Africa and the Legacy of Late Colonialism*, Princeton: Princeton University Press

Manji, F. & Carol O'Coill, 2002, 'The missionary position: NGOs and development in Africa' in *International Affairs* 78,3:567-83

Mboya, T., *Freedom and After, 1963*, London: Andre Deutsch

Mkandawire, T. & C. C. Soludo, eds., 1999, *Our Continent, Our Future: African Perspectives on Structural Adjustment*, Dakar: CODESRIA

Murphy, B. K., 2001, 'International NGOs and the challenge of modernity', in Deborah Eade & Ernst Ligteringen eds., *Debating Development*, Oxford: Oxfam GB

Mwaikusa, J. T., 1995, *Towards Responsible Democratic Government: Executive Power and Constitutional Practice in Tanzania, 1962-1992*, Ph.D., Dissertation, University of London

Nkrumah, K. 1965, *Neo-colonialism: The Last Stage of Imperialism*, London: Heinemann

Nyerere, J. K. 1963b, 'The Second Scramble', reprinted in Nyerere op. cit. 1967

Nyerere, J. K. 1968, *Freedom and Socialism*, London: Oxford University Press

Nyerere, J. K., 1967, *Freedom and Unity: A Selection from Writings and Speeches*, Dar es Salaam: Oxford University Press

Nyerere, J. K, 1963a, 'A United States of Africa', *Journal of Modern African Studies*, January 1963, Cambridge reprinted in Nyerere op. cit. 1967

Nyerere, J.K. 1966, 'The Dilemma of the Pan-Africanist,' in J. K. Nyerere, op. cit. 1968

Nyerere, J.K. 1997, 'Africa Must Unite', edited excerpts from a public lecture delivered in Accra to mark Ghana's fortieth Independence Day anniversary celebrations, United New Africa Global Network, <http://www.unitednewafrica.com/Africa%20Unite.htm>

Nyong'o, Ghirmazion & Lamba, eds. 2002, *New Partnership for Africa's Development, NEPAD: A New Path?* Nairobi: Heinrich Boll Foundation

Peacock, A., 2002, *Two Hundred Pharaohs and Five Billion Slaves*, London

Rodney, W. 1972, *How Europe Underdeveloped Africa*, Dar es Salaam: Tanzania Publishing House

Sayers, D., 1991, *Capitalism & Modernity: An Excursus on Marx and Weber*, London: Routledge

Semboja, J., Juma, Mwapachu & Eduard Jansen eds., 2002. *Local Perspectives on Globalisation: The African Case*, Dar es Salaam: REPOA & Mkuki na Nyota Publishers.

Sheriff, A., 1987, *Slaves, Spices & Ivory in Zanzibar*, London: James Curry

Shivji, I. G., 1987, 'The roots of the agrarian crisis in Tanzania,' *Eastern Africa Social Science Research Review*, vol. 111, no.1:111-134

Shivji, I. G., ed, 1991, *State and Constitutionalism: An African Debate on Democracy*, Harare: SAPES

Shivji, I. G., 1998, *Not Yet Democracy: Reforming Land Tenure in Tanzania*, London: IIED

Shivji, I. G. 2000, 'Critical Elements of a New Democratic Consensus in Africa' in Haroub Othman (ed.) *Reflections on Leadership in Africa: Essays in Honour of Mwalimu Julius K. Nyerere*, (Belgium: VUB University Press)

Shivji, I.G., 2002, 'Globalisation and Popular Resistance' in Joseph Semboja, Juma Mwapachu & Eduard Jansen, eds. *Local Perspectives on Globalisation: The African Case*, Dar es Salaam: REPOA, Mkuki na Nyota

Shivji, I. G., 2003, 'Three generations of constitutions and constitution-making in Africa: An overview and assessment in social and economic context', in M. S. Rosen ed., *Constitutionalism in Transition: Africa and Eastern Europe*, Helsinki Foundation for Human Rights

Shivji, I. G. 2005a, 'The Rise, the Fall and the Insurrection of Nationalism in Africa', in Felicia Arudo Yieke ed. op.cit.

Shivji, I.G., 2005b, 'Pan-Africanism or Imperialism?' 2nd Billy Dudley Memorial Lecture to the Nigerian Political Science Association, Nsukka, Nigeria, July 2005

Tandon, Y., 1982, University of Dar es Salaam: *Debate on Class, State & Imperialism*, Dar es Salaam: Tanzania Publishing House

Wamba, E., 1991, 'Discourse on the National Question', in I. G. Shivji, ed. *State and Constitutionalism: An African Debate on Democracy*, Harare: SAPES

Wamba, E., 1996, 'The National Question in Zaire: Challenges to the Nation-State Project', in Adebayo O. Olukoshi & Liisa Laakso, eds. *Challenges to the Nation-State in Africa*, Uppsala: Nordic African Institute

Williams, E., 1945, *Capitalism or Slavery*, London: Lomgman

Wilson, A., 1989, *US Foreign Policy and Revolution: The Creation of Tanzania*, London: Pluto

Yieke, F. A. ed. 2005, *East Africa: In Search of National and Regional Renewal*, Dakar: CODESRIA

# II

# Reflections on NGOs in Tanzania: What We Are, What We Are Not and What We Ought To Be[1]

## Issa G. Shivji

### SOUL-SEARCHING

We do not get many opportunities to sit back and reflect on ourselves as civil society activists. Reflecting on who we are, what are we doing and where we are going does not require any justification. In this age of imperial hegemony, transmitted to the peoples of the world through both state and non-state agencies, it is even more important that we create opportunities and consciously ask ourselves fundamental questions: Are we serving the best interests of our working people? Are we contributing to the great cause of humanity, the cause of emancipation from oppression, exploitation and deprivation? Or are we engaged, consciously or unconsciously, in playing to the tune set by others?

It is in this spirit of self-criticism, reflection and soul-searching that I want to offer a few thoughts, which I hope we can discuss honestly.

### OUR LIMITATIONS

To understand NGOs better, we must start by asking what we are, what we are not, and what our limitations are. Firstly, most of our NGOs are top-down organizations led by the elite. What is more, most of them are urban-based. In our case, NGOs did not begin as a response to the expressed need of the large majority of working people. It is true that many of us working in NGOs are well-intentioned. We want to contribute to some cause. However, we may define it. It is also true that some NGOs do address some of the real concerns of the working people.

[1] This paper was originally given as a keynote address to the Gender Festival organised by the Tanzania Gender Networking Group in September 2003. I am grateful to Natasha Shivji for reading and commenting on the draft.

Yet, we must recognize that we did not develop as, nor have we managed to become, organic to the mass of the people, at least so far. The relationship between the NGOs and the masses, therefore, remains, at best, that of benefactors and beneficiaries. There are better relationships than this when it comes to genuine activism with, rather than for, the people.

Secondly, we are not constituency or membership-based organizations. Even if we have a membership, this largely constitutes fellow elite members. Our accountability, therefore, is limited and limited to a small group of people. In fact, we may end up being more accountable to the donors who fund us than to our members, let alone our people.

Third, we are funded by and rely almost exclusively on foreign funding. This is the greatest single limitation. 'He who pays the piper calls the tune' holds true, however much we may wish to think otherwise. In many direct and subtle ways, those who fund us determine our agenda or place limits on or reorient them. Very few of us can really resist the pressures that external funding imposes on us.

In the NGO world, we have been raised to believe that we should act and not theorize. Theorization is detested. The result is that most 'NGO-wallahs' do not have any grand vision of society. Nor are they guided by large issues. Rather they concentrate on small, day-to-day matters. In NGOs, we hardly spend any time defining our vision in relation to the overall social and economic context of our societies.

Many of us tend to conflate NGOs with civil society organizations, thus undermining the traditional member and class-based organizations of the working people, such as trade unions and peasant associations. We may pay lip service to people's organizations, but in practice, both our benefactors – the so-called donor community – and we ourselves privilege NGOs. This has had far-reaching consequences, including undermining people's organizations.

Despite these limitations, NGOs can play a worthy role. But we do have to recognize what we are not. In the current context of neoliberal imperialist hegemony, NGOs have been cast in a surrogate role in our country, which many of us have come to accept. We may even feel flattered. This is where our limitations have been compounded. There is a danger that we assume a role that belongs to someone else, so we fail to play the role for which we may best be suited. This will become clearer as I examine some of our recent experiences of activism.

## PARTICIPATION BY SUBSTITUTION

As they developed in the West, NGOs were pressure groups to keep those in power, the state and the government, on their toes. In our case, as donors became disenchanted with states, they took a fancy to NGOs, thus undermining the state and its institutions while at the same time placating their own domestic constituencies demanding civil society involvement.

Participation and consultation are supposedly part of 'good governance', insisted on by donors, and allowing the imperial countries to legitimize the neoliberal policies of dominant Western powers and the international financial institutions (IFIs) in our countries.

NGOs are cast in the role of 'partners': partners of the state, partners of the erstwhile donor community, development partners, and partners in good governance. We get involved in so-called policy dialogues in which the triad of NGOs, government and donor representatives participate. We attend workshops as stakeholders. Donors who fund policymaking and their consultants who make policies seek us out for consultation. All this passes for people's participation and involvement, or so-called 'good governance'. But what is the implication of this type of participation for democratic governance in our countries?

One of the core functions and responsibilities of a government is policymaking in the interest of its people. It is emphatically not the function of donors. Donor-driven policymaking shows how much our states and people have lost the right to self-determination under the imperialist domination of the post-Cold War period, euphemistically called globalization.

By participating in this process, NGOs lend legitimacy to this domination. In fact, NGOs ought to be playing exactly the opposite role. NGOs can only possibly be fighting in the people's interest if they are in a position to expose and oppose imperial domination. The right to self-determination is our basic right as a people, as a nation, and as a country. It is the right for which our independence fighters laid down their lives. Now we seem to be legitimizing the process of losing it.

By pretending to be partners in policymaking, NGOs let the government off the hook as it abdicates its primary responsibility. The role of NGOs ought to be that of a watchdog, critiquing shortcomings in government policies and their implementation.

NGOs must do more than substitute themselves for the people. They are neither the elected representatives of the people nor mandated to represent them. Participation in the institutions of the state is the democratic right of all peoples. It ought to be done continuously by structuring appropriate legal, institutional and social frameworks.

As pressure and advocacy groups, our primary duty as NGOs is to pressure the powers that be to create conditions that enable the participation of the people themselves in the institutions of policymaking. This means our role should be to struggle to expand space for the people and people's organizations in the representative institutions of the state, such as parliament, local government councils, and village and neighborhood bodies.

The process of reforming and reconstituting the state in a democratic direction is the only way to ensure genuine popular participation and to deter abuse of state power. This is a continuous process of struggle and cannot be reduced to some one-off ad hoc process of stakeholder workshops and policy dialogues.

If the struggle for democratic reform were thus conceived, then the strategy itself of the NGOs would change. There would be protracted public debates instead of stakeholder conferences and the development of alternative ways of doing things instead of so-called inputs into consultants' policy drafts. There would be demonstrations, protest marches and teach-ins in streets and community centers to expose serious abuses of power and bad policies instead of the so-called policy dialogues in five-star hotels. Democratic governance would be an arena where power is contested, not some moral dialogue or crusade for good against evil, as the meaningless term 'good governance' implies. You cannot dialogue with power.

In short, I urge that we must re-examine our conceptualization and practice of the new and fancy roles of partners and stakeholders we are being given. We cannot possibly be partners and hold a stake in a system that oppresses and dehumanizes the large majority of people.

## SELECTIVE ACTIVISM

The great strength of the NGOs is supposed to be their consistent, principled and committed stand for human values and causes in the interest of the popular masses. We are not a bunch of self-seeking petty-bourgeois politicians who are inconsistent, almost by definition, driven more by power than principles. We, activists, are not in the business of brokering power where expediency and compromise rule. Our business is to resist and expose the ugly face of power. We are guided, and our work is informed by deeply held human values and causes. Consistency of principles and commitment to humanity should inform all our work, thought, activism and advocacy.

Our values and causes may be summed as three elements, which I have elsewhere called popular livelihoods, popular participation and popular power.[2] Whether expressed in the language of democracy or human rights, most of our values and causes can be summed up in these three elements. By 'popular' I mean to refer to the exploited and oppressed classes and groups in our society. This contrasts with the current, utterly demeaning and singularly useless neoliberal discourse

---

[2] See Issa Shivji, 2000, 'Critical Elements of a New Democratic Consensus in Africa' in Othman, H. (ed) *Reflections on Leadership in Africa: Forty Years after Independence*, Belgium: VUB Brussels University Press, 2000

in which popular classes are dubbed the 'poor', to be incessantly researched upon, and targeted to receive poverty alleviation funds.

The term 'popular' is meant to signify the central place of the working people in the struggle to regain their livelihoods, dignity and power. I shall not go into details about these concepts here. Suffice it to say that I believe these elements signify the values and causes with which many NGOs and activists identify. I contend that many of our NGOs have consistently failed to stand up for these values and have thereby greatly compromised themselves. Let me cite three recent experiences. I am doing this as a matter of critical reflection rather than pointing fingers.

In 2003 the whole world was shaken to the core, and basic human values were cynically challenged when the United States invaded and occupied Iraq. Millions of people all over the world demonstrated and protested in great defiance of this monstrosity – as individuals, as NGO activists, and as simple decent human beings. Here in Dar es Salaam, our NGO world was shamefully silent. A small demonstration organized by the university student union attracted a few NGOs and activists. But well-known human rights NGOs and advocates were conspicuous in their absence. The umbrella NGO organizations did not so much as issue a simple statement, either on their own or in solidarity with others. How can we who espouse democratic values of freedom and self-determination explain such silence?

Let us take the second example. When our government was debating the NGO bill, one of the most draconian bills, the so-called 'anti-terrorism law', was being discussed. The NGO bill was rightly opposed by NGOs. One may critique their strategy. That is another matter for another occasion. The point here is that these same NGOs were utterly silent on the anti-terrorism bill. In South Africa and Kenya, NGOs were at the forefront of opposition to the anti-terrorism law. To their credit, our sister NGOs in Kenya have put up such stiff resistance that the bill has not yet been passed. But ours sailed through parliament. Many people are asking and are entitled to ask: how come? Are we NGOs selective in the freedoms we support? Was our cowardly silence in respect of the anti-terrorism law because our benefactors include the likes of USAID? Is it because we are just like any other self-seeking group in that we readily challenged the NGO bill that threatened our own existence while conveniently ignoring the anti-terrorism law, which delivers a shattering blow to all basic freedoms and rights?

Indeed, NGOs cannot do everything and be everywhere. But the question of Iraq and the spate of anti-terrorism laws and measures thrust down the throats of our government and people is not just anything. It marks an important turning point in the establishment of imperial hegemony of the single superpower with far-reaching consequences for the freedoms, rights, dignity and independence of the peoples of the world, particularly the Third World.

Under the pretext of fighting terrorism, the superpower is involved in changing the world map. It is playing god by deciding for us what is good and what is evil. It is establishing a string of training colleges for spies and new types of police on the continent, including in our own country. Yet, the NGO world sleeps soundly. Latin America knows and has experienced what happens when you have your forces of 'law and order' trained in methods of disappearances, mysterious murders and pre-emptive killings of those labeled 'terrorists'. A whole people – those we used to call freedom fighters, liberators and organic intellectuals of the people – become non-people! Witness the atrocities Central and Latin American people suffered, from El Salvador to Nicaragua, from Argentina to Chile. Many perpetrators of these horrendous crimes were 'trained' in the so-called School of the Americas, sponsored by the notorious CIA. Surely, no NGO worth its salt can ignore the lessons from other continents and stand on the sidelines whilst the seeds of instability are planted on our continent?

## SOLIDARITY WITH PEOPLE'S ORGANIZATIONS

In the 1980s and 1990s, many activists enthusiastically struggled for the opening organizational space for the people. That was when NGOs mushroomed, and the multi-party system was introduced. Coming out of the background of the domination of the authoritarian state, which killed and maimed people's independent organizational initiatives, it is quite understandable that we were at the forefront of the struggle for the independence of civil society. Yet, in the larger context of the moral and ideological rehabilitation of imperialism in the post-Cold War era, NGOs appear to have undermined traditional people's organizations, just as human rights ideology has displaced ideologies of national liberation and social emancipation.

Many NGOs have failed to realize this. Therefore, they may be lending credence to this process without being necessarily conscious of it.

As the third example, let us look at trade unions in our country. The trade union movement was first suppressed in 1964, before political parties in 1965. Freedom to form political parties was reintroduced in 1992; freedom to form trade unions came only in 1998. Since then, against very strong odds and under adverse conditions, the trade unions have struggled to establish themselves as truly class and constituency-based organizations.

Privatization and globalization have greatly undermined the efforts of the working class. It is being decimated through redundancy and impoverished as public social services such as water, sanitation, education, electricity and healthcare are turned into private commodities for sale on the market in the interest of private profit.

Nonetheless, the fledgling trade unions have been involved in a desperate struggle against the new exploiters, the so-called wawekezaji. This includes South African capital, which is moving north ferociously in its second round of primitive accumulation on the continent. We have witnessed the saga of the workers of the National Bank of Commerce (NBC). What is interesting and inexplicable is that the NGOs played no role at all in these struggles, not even expressing solidarity.

As long as the NGOs participate in stakeholder workshops discussing poverty alleviation strategy papers, they seem to be oblivious to the creation of poverty through redundancy and the robbery of public goods as social services are privatized. When the NBC workers held their mass meetings, sister trade unions sent delegations to express solidarity. I did not see or hear of any NGO doing the same.

A lack of understanding amongst the NGOs of our correct place and role in the struggles of the working people manifests itself on other levels. There have been massive anti-globalization and anti-capitalist movements in the West. But again, our presence there could be more prominent. In our own situation, the Lawyers Environmental Action Team (LEAT)[3] has been involved in a protracted exposure of the abuses of the mining companies. But our NGOs and their umbrella organizations have remained quiet. We have not uttered even a word of solidarity, let alone held demonstrations and protests in militant solidarity.

## CONCLUSION: ARTICULATING AN ACTIVIST WORLD VIEW AND CHOOSING SIDES

We, the NGOs and activists, should look at ourselves hard. We must take stock of our activities. We must evaluate ourselves in the light of our values, principles and mission to create a better world. If an alternative world is indeed possible – and it is – we need to know our existing world. Not only knowing the existing world but also knowing who is running it. Why and how does the existing world keep reproducing itself? In whose interest? For what purpose? And we must choose sides: the side of those who are struggling for a better world against those who want to maintain the existing world. Put simply, we cannot be neutral.

The question facing us is: Can we better understand the existing world to create a better world without a grand vision, a grand theory, or a worldview rooted in the experiences of the working people? Can

---

3 See https://www.leat.or.tz

we really eschew thinking, theorizing and knowing? The dominant powers and their spokespersons speak of the 'end of history' and the 'end of ideology'. They tell us the age of solidarity with the oppressed peoples is gone. We are told: now is the age of economics, not politics.

Our leaders tell us there is only one world: the existing world, the globalized world, the hegemonic world. 'Either sink or swim', they say. The truth of the matter is that the working people are sinking in the globalized world while the elite are swimming in it. It is clear, therefore, that there is a contest between two worldviews: one that wants to maintain the existing world, the other that wants to create an alternative world. Which worldview do we share? We must make a choice and act in accordance with our choice.

Let me end with two very poignant quotations broadly representing the two worldviews in a specific context. A story in The Guardian reporting on the new Tanzanian foreign policy claimed it stressed economic interests rather than political considerations. At the end of the story, the US ambassador, speaking to the Parliamentary Committee for Foreign Affairs on 29 July 2003, is quoted. Commending Tanzania for its new 'economic diplomacy', he says:

> The liberation diplomacy of the past, when alliances with socialist nations were paramount and so-called Third World solidarity dominated foreign policy, must give way to a more realistic approach to dealing with your true friends - those who are working to lift you into the 21st century where poverty is not acceptable and disease must be conquered.

Some 30 years ago, former independence leader and president of Tanzania Mwalimu Nyerere, commenting about the need to change another 'realistic' world – apartheid South Africa – said:

> Humanity has already passed through many phases since man began his evolutionary journey. And nature shows us that not all life evolves in the same way. The chimpanzees - to whom once we were very near - got on to the wrong evolutionary path and they got stuck. And there were other species which became extinct; their teeth were so big, or their bodies so heavy, that they could not adapt to changing circumstances and they died out.
>
> I am convinced that, in the history of the human race, imperialists and racialists will also become extinct. They are now very powerful. But they are a very primitive animal. The only difference between them and these other extinct creatures is that their teeth and claws are more elaborate and cause much greater harm ...
>
> But failure to co-operate together is a mark of bestiality; it is not a characteristic of humanity. Imperialists and racialists will go. Vorster, and all like him, will come to an end. Every racialist in the

world is an animal of some kind or the other, and all are kinds that have no future. Eventually they will become extinct. Africa must refuse to be humiliated, exploited, and pushed around. And with the same determination we must refuse to humiliate, exploit, or push others around. We must act, not just say words.[4]

The pundits of the status quo have in common with all dominating classes and hegemonic powers the assumption that the existing world is the only realistic world and that no alternative world is possible. Yet, the struggle for an alternative world, a better one, has changed the past and will continue to change the present for a better future. We, the activists, together with the working people, must continue to fight for a better world. An alternative world is possible.

---

[4] Julius Nyerere, 1973, *Freedom and Development: A Selection from Writings and Speeches*, Oxford University Press, p.371

# TITLES OF INTEREST FROM DARAJA PRESS

**Kenyan Organic Intellectuals
Reflect on the Legacy of Pio Gama Pinto**
ISBN 9781990263323

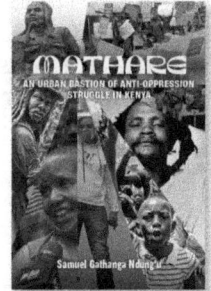

**Mathare: An Urban Bastion of
Anti-Oppression Struggle in Kenya**
Samuel Gathanga Ndung'u
ISBN 9781990263422

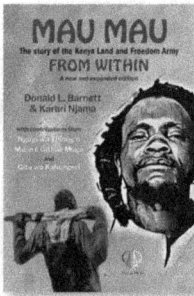

**Mau Mau From Within: The Story of
the Kenya Land and Freedom Army**
Donald Barnett & Karari Njama
ISBN 9781988832593

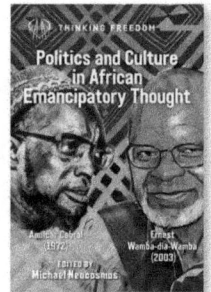

**Politics and Culture
in African Emancipatory Thought**
Amilcar Cabral, Ernest Wamba-Dia-Wamba,
Michael Neocosmos
ISBN 9781990263330

**Life Histories from the Revolution:
Three militants from the Kenya Land and
Freedom Army tell their stories**
Karigo Muchai, Mohamed Mathu, Ngugi Kabiru
ISBN 9781990263132

**From Citizen to Refugee:**
**Uganda Asians come to Britain**
Mahmood Mamdani
ISBN 9781990263514

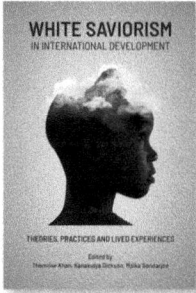

**The White Savior Complex in International Development:**
**Theories, Practices and Lived Experiences**
Themrise Khan, Kanakulya Dickson and Maïka Sondarjee
ISBN 9781990263187

**We Rise for Our Land:**
**Land Struggles and Repression in Southern Africa**
Boaventura Monjane
ISBN 9781988832685

**Decolonization and Afro-Feminism**
Sylvia Tamale
ISBN 9781988832494

**Poems for the Penniless**
Issa G Shivji
ISBN 9781988832173

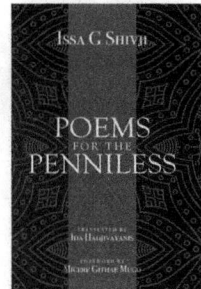

Order from **darajapress.com** or **zandgraphics.com**

Daraja Press